# PRAISE FOR WHAT BLACK PARENTS NEEDS TO KNOW ABOUT SAVING OUR SONS

"It is always heartening to see women step up to the writer's table. When the results are as adroit and affecting as Marita Golden's work, it is more than satisfying; it is a cause for celebration."

—Toni Morrison, Nobel Laureate

"Marita Golden has captured the special pain that shadows the joy of Black parenthood in these turbulent times. Elegantly written, this book is a breakthrough."

—*Chicago Tribune*

"A wonderful storyteller, an uncompromising mind, Marita Golden explores the African-American experience in a completely original way."

—*Newsweek*

"In this book, Marita reminds us why every black parent should be vigilant and intentional in considering how to steer young black boys—and girls as well—through the precarious passage to adulthood. *Saving Our Sons* is disturbingly relevant in this, the twenty-first century. It's a compelling read."

—Nathan McCall, author of *Makes Me Wanna Holler: A Young Black Man in America*

# What Every Black Parent Needs to Know About Saving Our Sons

# What Every Black Parent Needs to Know About Saving Our Sons

INSTITUTIONALIZED RACISM, SOCIETY, AND RAISING BLACK CHILDREN

## Marita Golden

CORAL GABLES

For permission requests, please contact the publisher at:

Mango Publishing Group

2850 S Douglas Road, 4th Floor

Coral Gables, FL 33134 USA

info@mango.bz

For special orders, quantity sales, course adoptions and corporate sales, please email the publisher at sales@mango.bz. For trade and wholesale sales, please contact Ingram Publisher Services at customer.service@ingramcontent.com or +1.800.509.4887.

*What Every Black Parent Needs to Know About Saving Our Sons: Institutionalized Racism, Society, and Raising Black Children*

Library of Congress Cataloging-in-Publication number: 2023945045

ISBN: (pb) 978-1-68481-414-5 (e) 978-1-68481-473-2

BISAC category code SOC031000, SOCIAL SCIENCE / Discrimination

Printed in the United States of America

This book is for my son, Michael, with thanks for growing with me, for the generosity of his spirit, and for allowing me to reveal his life to others as the gift I have always known it was.

"The strongest lesson I can teach my son is the same lesson I teach my daughter: how to be who he wishes to be for himself. And this means how to move to that voice from within himself, rather than to those raucous, persuasive, or threatening voices from outside, pressuring him to be what the world wants him to be."

—Audre Lorde

"No black mother grows up in this city or any city without fearing for her son...No black mother doesn't fear. I don't think a black person can get away from it."

—Sylvia Snowden (mother of Malik Butler, who was murdered on a Washington, DC, street corner)

# Table of Contents

# Publisher's Note

## PROTECTING OUR COLLECTIVE FUTURE

One of the books I am most proud to publish is this essential parenting book by the wise and wonderful Marita Golden. Parenting is hard work; you have to raise your child and teach them how to succeed as an independent adult. This is simply not enough for parents of Black sons in America; you must also prepare them to face racial inequity of all kinds. They need to know how to navigate a world where the odds are so often stacked against them, from microaggressions at school to macroaggressions that can end with a gun aimed at you during a routine traffic stop. While society is working toward a level playing field for Black families, we have a long way to go. That is why I am honored to have worked on Golden's book, which faces these problems head-on and offers helpful information, tough and honest talk, and an abundance of resources for kids and parents. In this new edition, the incredible M.J. Fievre offers her wisdom on preparing your Black sons to survive and thrive in her afterword that includes "The Talk" and many more vital tips and suggestions. As the author of *Raising Confident Black Kids*, M.J. offers so much to Black families. Perhaps the most important thing about this book is that it offers tools and, while realistic, is never hopeless but hews toward that better future.

We would love to hear from you too, and I invite you to contact me directly at my email below. I hope this book helps you on your journey, and I wish you all the best and a life filled with awesomeness.

Be well,
**Brenda Knight**
Publisher, Mango Publishing Group
Brenda@MangoPublishingGroup.com

# Foreword

I met Marita Golden years ago when I was a reporter for the *Washington Post*. At the time, I was learning my way around Washington, DC. Marita moved among a flourishing group of Black writers in the city. In our encounters at cultural events around town and through reading her work, I saw Marita's passion for exploring the human condition, not only as a writer, but also as a world citizen.

I had been a fan of Marita's work since reading her first book, *Migrations of the Heart*. It was a searing account of her marriage to a Nigerian man and her subsequent relocation with him to the Motherland. In her four years living in Nigeria, she birthed a son and grew to appreciate an experience that most African Americans only dream of—living in a nation where Blackness is the norm. In *Migrations of the Heart*, Marita also chronicled the cultural and gender-related clashes with her husband that ultimately doomed her marriage and drove her to return to the United States.

It was apparent from *Migrations* and the books that followed that Marita's work as an artist reflects a drive to examine issues and seek answers to some of Black Americans' most pressing concerns. So it came as no surprise when her focus landed on her young son who, as a young Black male, inherited the dubious distinction of being labeled an endangered species in America. This book, *Saving Our Sons: Raising Black Children in a Turbulent World,* is the story of how Marita, then a single mother, set out with a fierce determination to raise an African-American boy in a country hostile to his very existence.

There is an obvious irony that made *Saving Our Sons* seem like an extension of *Migrations of the Heart*: Marita was struck by the fact that in Nigerian society, sons are held in high esteem. In America, however, the opposite is true. Black males are generally devalued and often treated as cogs in a nefarious school-to-prison-pipeline, where sizeable head counts bring vast profits on the New York Stock Exchange.

Year after year, the data about Black boys' prospects in life yields distressing news: Black boys are more likely than their white peers to be expelled from school. Black boys are more likely than others to be committed to detention centers for juvenile infractions. Homicide is a leading cause of death among Black males under the age of twenty-one.

Marita, faced with such a daunting reality, squarely confronted the probabilities of what might happen if she failed to help her son, Michael, navigate the pitfalls that awaited him, not only in the mean streets, but also in virtually every white-run institution that he would encounter over the years as he tried to find his way in America.

For me as a Black man, *Saving Our Sons* resonated in ways that are deeply personal. In a sense, I represent the embodiment of the nightmare that Marita hoped to avert in raising her son. I wrote about my journey in my autobiography, *Makes Me Wanna Holler: A Young Black Man in America*. I chronicled my passage from being a smart kid in elementary school to a corner boy by the time I reached junior high. Before all was said and done, I had shot a man in the chest at point-blank range and later committed an armed robbery that resulted in a twelve-year prison sentence.

As Marita noted in *Saving Our Sons*, such tragedies don't exist in a vacuum; they impact entire families and often sweep like cyclones through whole communities. I eventually managed to recover from my travails, but not before inflicting a great deal of collateral pain on my family and on others.

*Saving Our Sons* resonated with me for another reason as well. In Marita's story I came to better understand my own mother's anguished attempts to save me from the streets, from the system, and from myself. For all her maternal love and effort, my mom lacked the skills and vocabulary to forge the tough, often awkward conversations between parents and children that are so vital. Conversely, Marita forced herself to push beyond her comfort zone and engaged her son in discussions that challenged distorted schoolyard notions about sex, violence, manhood, and more that competed for space in his head. Additionally, she sought the help of experts and regular people whose lived experiences might offer critical insights on Black boys. And she enlisted the aid of the proverbial "village"—people in her community who could help reinforce positive images and messages.

*Saving Our Sons* is not some sterile account from an academic theorizing from the relative safety of the ivory tower. This is a deeply passionate account from a Black woman reporting from the front lines of a struggle that strikes at the very heart of Black survival.

In this book, Marita reminds us why every Black parent should be vigilant and intentional in considering how to steer young Black boys—and girls as well—through the precarious passage to adulthood.

*Saving Our Sons* is disturbingly relevant in this, the twenty-first century. It's a compelling read.

—Nathan McCall, author of *Makes Me Wanna Holler: A Young Black Man in America*

# Introduction

So much in the lives of African Americans has evolved and changed in the decades since the first edition of *Saving Our Sons*. A Black president, a Black woman Supreme Court justice, and yet, as I write this, state legislators, local and state courts, and the Supreme Court are overturning decades of progress in the fight for equality. Today's parents of Black children have the same responsibility to their children as previous generations of parents. The assignment? Helping our children to understand the society and world they are part of, to recognize their worth, and to be part of making this world a better place for everyone. And showing them how to protect themselves as much as they can from physical and mental harm in a society that is often designed to undermine them and their well-being. And most importantly, I want Black children to know that they have a right to innocence, joy, and happiness. Let's show our children how to recognize and cherish the love of their families and communities, and to love themselves.

Black parents of necessity want and need to have conversations with their children that they hope will save their lives. All conversations, especially with Black males but increasingly with all of our children, begin and end with *The Talk,* the conversation that Black families have about how to conduct oneself during a police stop to ensure one's survival. This is the post-George Floyd, the post-Sandra Bland generation, so *The Talk* has become a kind of verbal insurance policy extended by Black parents to all their children, not just males. In the age of police video dash cams, cell phone cameras, and the acceptance of videos as legitimate documentation of police stops, Black parents know that the rules of *The Talk* are still relevant and have not changed much. Those rules recommend actions that will de-escalate potential tension with police officers, because so many poorly trained, aggressive, or racist police officers of any race lack de-escalation training or skills. *The Talk* is as necessary today as in the past. My husband and I had *The Talk* with Michael, and I would have the same conversation today with any Black child in my care. Experts recommend telling your child to remain calm if stopped by the police, comply with all requests, do not flee, and, if they are asked for more information than name and address, request the presence of a parent or lawyer and realize that any improprieties can be dealt with after the stop.

* * *

When I was raising my son, I worked hard to instill in him a sense of pride in his heritage both as a Black American and as the son of a Nigerian father. My son was in the most literal and figurative senses an African American. I was raised by a father who was an old-fashioned "race-man," and it was from him that I learned most of what I knew as a child about Black history. Today I would include conversations and lessons with Michael about systemic racism, what it is, how to identify it, how to fight it, and how to work to dismantle it. No longer is Black pride sufficient for Black children. Black pride must be wedded to knowledge about how racism impacts their lives, from the police stop to the job interview, to the classroom. We must talk to Black children about systemic racism, while avoiding instilling them with a sense that they are born victims or that systemic racism is immutable and inevitable. We need to tell our children that backlash and resistance are part of progress, and that backlash cannot stop progress.

I wanted to raise Michael to be a proud Black man who was intelligent, creative, generous, and humane. Today in addition, I would want my son to be an active change agent, no matter what profession he chose. I write this post-Trump and possibly pre-Trump again. I write this in the midst of unprecedented daily gun violence and a nation of locked and loaded and fearful-of-Black-people Whites and too many young Black men locked and loaded too. I feel the need to arm my son with tools that can possibly ensure his survival against assault from the seen, the known, and the unknown. Tragically these family conversations are as necessary as active-shooter trainings in many of this country's public schools, colleges, universities, businesses, and churches. Hate is increasingly taking literal aim at African Americans, Jewish people, and LGBTQ+ individuals. Our children need to know how systemic racism, bigotry, and marginalization work and what they can do to respond to it and change it.

I would talk with my son about the evolutionary ways in which we are experiencing and defining gender, gender roles, and sexuality. I would tell my son that many of the iterations of gender identity becoming public are ancient and have been part of the human experience for millennia in cultures around the world. I would tell my son that how people express their gender and sexuality in no way proscribes or dilutes their humanity and that we are bound to one another by our humanity, a humanity that is multi-dimensional and that is much more than our genitals or even who we choose to love. African Americans are disproportionately discriminated against in cases of gender bias. And so, this is an issue that I hope will inspire him to be informed, reflective, and humane. African Americans identifying as LGBTQ+, and especially trans, are subject to higher levels of discrimination.

I would have continuous and continuing conversations with my son about social media and Artificial Intelligence. He has to be more than a consumer of these powerful expressions of the marketplace and technology. I would learn how to play video games and become familiar with the most popular games, and especially the games my son played. For some parents, this might seem to be asking too much, but you can't honestly discuss or critique what you are unfamiliar with. I would talk with my son about how important it is not to be held hostage by social media and the need to spend more time in the real world than the virtual world. And, as his parent, I would enact "house rules" for when and where social media could be part of family life. Simultaneously, I would hope to instill a respect for technological milestones. As a product of humans, Artificial Intelligence is burdened and encoded with biases of all kinds, but it also offers hope for progress in many ways. In the world that today's young Black youth will inhabit, this will offer new opportunities and, unless radically altered, generations-old challenges to equity.

* * *

I would talk with my son about the importance of recognizing that true health includes caring for mental health. Young people coming of age today are much more open to disclosing, recognizing, and treating mental health challenges than previous generations. They need to know that they have family support when they feel the need to seek professional mental health care. If as a parent I have been in therapy or mental health counseling of any kind, I would speak openly and candidly about the experience with my child so that they feel comfortable and supported when they face issues like anxiety or depression.

I conclude, as I began, with the recommendation of joy as a crucial element of parenting Black children. Our children are not *the problem;* they are not a *problem.* Rather our children live in a society that makes their health and well-being deeply problematic. Because of that definition, instilling in our children the ability to celebrate life and who they are is essential. That talent for celebration, no matter what, sustained their ancestors, and it will and can sustain them.

# Calling My Name

At a corner table in an upscale restaurant heavy on redwood paneling, scented candles, and a retro sixties atmosphere, Elaine Ellis Comegys and I sat talking about sons. I was a visiting writer in residence at Antioch College in Yellow Springs, Ohio, where Elaine is an associate dean of students. At noon we had set out, walking leisurely from the nearby campus to this restaurant located in "downtown," an area that is really no more than a five-block strip of retailers which include a gourmet carryout place, a health food store, an art supply shop, a children's bookstore, and the town's only theater. Yellow Springs possesses a vaguely aging counterculture feel, and the town invoked in me fond memories of a time when my Afro hair was several inches thicker than the close, conservative natural I wore that day.

Ebullient and warm, Elaine had given me a capsule history of Yellow Springs, population 4,000, including its status as a stop on the Underground Railroad. In May 1993, the town was bucolic, lovely, and so safe that unlocked doors along the wide tree-lined, shaded streets were common. The most serious recent crime wave anyone could remember was one spawned by a serial bicycle thief.

Psychologically, I was a long way from Washington, DC, where I returned each Thursday evening to spend the weekend with my family. I would be spending a month at Antioch, teaching a workshop on autobiographical writing, and so during lunch that day, I gently grilled Elaine, in a sister-to-sister-on-a-white-campus way, to tell me everything she knew that I should know too. Over Elaine's pasta and my fish, we dredged up academic anecdotes. We had both spent much of our professional lives on historically white campuses, and so the revelations and headshaking lasted awhile. But by the time we ordered dessert, we were talking about sons, ours and everyone else's.

Elaine and I landed on the gritty shore of this topic, any resistance to it capsized by its inescapable pull on our emotions. For at that moment, it was the fate and the crisis of our sons that obsessed and engaged us. Whether we were talking about the schools, a drive-by shooting, the economy, rap music, or the Knicks versus the Bullets, we were really talking about our sons. We talked about them because if we had not yet lost them, we feared we would. And looking into each other's eyes, hearing the confusion in our own voices, we wondered who could tell us how to get them back.

Elaine recounted an incident involving a Black writer we both knew whose son was driving home one evening in their affluent, mostly white neighborhood outside New York City. Shortly before reaching home, the young man was stopped by two white policemen who had been following him and had signaled for him to pull over. When he stopped his car and the policemen approached him, they grilled the young man as to why he was in the neighborhood. His assertion that he lived six houses down the block was greeted with disbelief, brutal laughter, and threatened physical punishment. Then they ordered him out of the car and handcuffed him. In the process of roughing him up, the policemen injured the nerves in the fingers of the young man's right hand so badly that he suffered permanent damage. He only escaped arrest when his younger brother, studying in the living room, noticed the reflection of the twirling red lights on the picture window of their house. He then went outside to investigate and found his brother being held down against the hood of a police car by the two cops, still insisting that he was simply on his way home. Only when the young man's parents came to the scene was he released.

"She was devastated, as you can imagine," Elaine concluded with a weary sigh, stirring her coffee. Her gaze, like mine—which was reflected in her glasses—was confounded. "And when we talked a few days after it happened, she kept asking over and over, 'How could this happen to my son?' "

"There was no label on him certifying that he was educated, middle class, not a dangerous 'bad nigger,' " I said, the Rodney King tape flashing, quick and painful, through my brain. "And who knows, that probably would not have even mattered. His skin, that's the only label they saw."

Then I began an account of the day a group of boys with guns entered my son's junior high school and methodically searched classrooms looking for a boy with whom they wanted to permanently settle a score. My voice tensed at the memory of how calmly my son told my husband, Joe, and me of the incident over dinner, how proudly Michael detailed his early departure by a side entrance to avoid a stray bullet or the impending fight rumored to be scheduled for the park outside the school that afternoon. "How did it get so bad?" I asked Elaine wistfully. "What happened? How did we become the enemy too?"

We sat there, two educated, articulate women who prided themselves on their ability to navigate the tightrope stretched between the Black and the white worlds. Now that the talk of sons had started, we recounted one incident after another—the son of a friend caught in cross fire, the son of a cousin doing time in jail for selling drugs. Yet for all the verbiage exchanged that afternoon, we were unable to explain how we had arrived in this season of blood and ashes.

That was the spring I decided I would remove my son from public school in Washington, DC, and enroll him in a private boarding school outside Philadelphia, as much to save his life as to buy him a good education. And after a lifetime spent in the inner city, my husband was suddenly willing to look at houses in the suburbs when we decided we needed more space. Drug traffic, once banished from our street by a combination of neighborhood vigilance and police cooperation, had returned. My car was broken into and the radio stolen. We lived five blocks from Howard University, two blocks from the now-boarded-up Howard Theater, once a mecca for Black stars from Duke Ellington in the thirties to James Brown in the sixties. Now addicts and prostitutes congregated all day before the grim, battered shell that was all that remained of the theater. And two weeks before my residency at Antioch began, a murderer dubbed the "Shotgun Stalker," who had randomly killed four people in a neighborhood a mile from where we lived, was captured in a parking lot three blocks from our house.

That afternoon, as Elaine and I sipped our herbal tea and nibbled our chocolate mousse, and after we paid the bill and walked slowly, almost reluctantly, back to campus, homicide was the leading cause of death for young Black males. That reality sat, a visible, intruding ghost, in the restaurant with us, strode along the clean neat streets of Yellow Springs, lay in wait for us in our campus offices. That statistic, like so much else in Black life, is surrealistic, chilling, and outrageous. Somewhere between the fact that Black males are the prime victims of crime and violence and the false media-generated image that they are responsible as well for nearly all the crime in America lies the truth. But where and how do you find it?

As the mother of a Black son, I have raised my child with a trembling hand that clutches and leads. I am no slave mother, my sleep plundered by images of the auction block. I dream instead of my son slaying the statistics that threaten to ensnare and cripple him, statistics that I know are a commentary on the odds for my son, who isn't dead or in jail. And though I have paved a straight and narrow path for my son to tread, always there is the fear that he will make a fatal detour, be seduced, or be hijacked by a white or a Black cop, or a young Black predator, or a Nazi skinhead, or his own bad judgment, or a weakness that even I as his mother cannot love or punish or will out of him.

And yet I say defiantly, "They are all my sons," the young prodigals as well as the boys who keep the faith of Black mothers and fathers. Over dinner a few weeks earlier, my friend Debra had described her new job as head of public relations for one of the largest hospitals in Washington. As part of her training, she had spent an evening in Medstar, the hospital's nationally known trauma unit. She was clearly shaken as she recalled, "The evening I spent in the trauma unit was hell. I felt so bad watching them bring in one Black male after another, shot in the arm, wounded in the chest. I watched them use electrodes to try to get their hearts going again. It's as if everything I'd read in the papers meant nothing until I was in that room to see it up close."

Patty, a TV producer, shifted in her chair next to Debra and pronounced, with more precision and honesty than I could bear, "I've got a six-year-old boy, and I feel like I'm raising a target."

I am too smart and too skeptical to believe all the hype. I know that it is only a small percentage of males in the Black community who have planted this terror we feel. But no matter how I add the numbers and take the pulse of my neighbors and friends, I know that African Americans inhabit a literal and figurative space unlike anything in our previous experience.

At a party one night, a journalist friend proudly said, "Look at all those white kids who get drunk and speed to their deaths in the suburbs, or their fathers who wake up one morning and shoot the whole family. We've no monopoly on violence."

"Maybe not, but proportionately, we've got a monopoly on death," I nearly screamed at him. "My husband is a high school teacher in Washington. How many teachers in Chevy Chase or Montgomery County can say, like him, that over a dozen students they've taught have been killed?" I was suddenly too weary to talk to my friend about the emotional toll of all this on my husband and his fellow teachers, as well as on their students, who had witnessed kids snuffed out literally before their eyes.

I have used language to decipher and overcome politically and culturally imposed madness. I have used words to claim sporadic cherished moments of beauty, real and imagined. And because all Black boys, the ones on the six-o'clock news in handcuffs and the ones singing in the church choir, are my sons, the sons of my community and the sons of America, I began searching for them that spring. I looked for our sons with a hunger that took root when my father first told me about my ancestors who built kingdoms and survived cotton fields; on the day my own son was born; and when the Black-on-Black violence began in earnest. Maybe, I thought, if I write long and hard and strongly and bravely enough, I can save and protect my son and somehow bless the others. This moment, when intraracial violence and death undermine any possibility for progress and complicate easy definitions of *The Problem* and *The Solution*, is a new kind of Middle Passage. What will we look like, how will we sound, once we are spewed forth from the terrible hold of *this* ship?

• • •

A few weeks before I began my residency at Antioch, Dr. Joyce Ladner, then vice president for academic affairs at Howard University, arranged for me to give a reading and lecture at Howard. A veteran civil rights worker who dodged bombs and bullets working for the Student Non-Violent Coordinating Committee in her home state of Mississippi, a nationally known sociologist, and the mother of a son, Ladner and I have known each other professionally for over twenty years. I have always profoundly respected her ability to capture and translate the voices of our young, whether it was the too-often hushed voices of young Black girls captured in her groundbreaking first book, *Tomorrow's Tomorrow*, or the bravado of young Black males on Washington's embattled streets whom she wrote about in a series for the *Washington Post*. After reading from one of my novels and answering questions in the chapel, I walked with Ladner across the Howard campus. The students we passed wore dreadlocks, fades, naturals, wigs, cornrows, African kente cloth, blue jeans, miniskirts; they were the first generation of Black people able to be "Black" any way they chose. Watching them, I wondered if they knew how much their parents, uncles, aunts, and generations of grandparents had "paid" for them to stride across the campus of a school, one at once historic and financially beleaguered, with a confidence they couldn't imagine not possessing. I mentioned to Ladner that I had decided to send my son to a private boarding school. I told her this because I remained conflicted. As a product of DC's public schools, I still believed in the ideal of public education and was haunted by the notion that I was copping out of the struggle and the race in making this choice.

"My son has been in boarding school for the past four years. He graduates in June." She beamed proudly as we reached my car. "I believe firmly that they are a valuable option. And I wish more Black parents could send their kids away."

I was surprised by her response, but as we continued to talk, Ladner spoke as a sociologist who had studied and witnessed the horrific impact of violence and crime in the Black community. For Joyce Ladner, boarding schools were simply a way of protecting Black kids from streets meaner than anything she or I ever knew.

I asked her what the trade-offs had been in sending her son away to school. "The first trade-off is he's *alive*," she said emphatically, the statement so stunning and assured I was momentarily left breathless. I wondered how many white women who were a stone's throw away from the presidency of a major university feared so much for their sons' safety that they could make a similar statement.

A daughter of the South, an intellectual, a scholar, a "sister," and still possessed of a soft, lilting Mississippi accent, when she recalls growing up in Hattiesburg, her voice is wistful and yearning. Ladner said that one of the primary reasons she chose a boarding school for her son was because "I wanted him to have a safe place to grow up, and I wanted him to have a nurturing, supportive community like the Black community that raised me in Mississippi." We talked about how growing up in the segregated South had shaped expectations and relations between Black men and women.

"Every generation of Black women has experienced tremendous anxiety about keeping their men alive," she said. Her words forced me to remember how frequently Black women are and have been leaders in the community, often brilliantly, by default, unrecognized and unrewarded. Now with the murders leaving widows, mothers of fatherless children, women who will never have men to marry, we have become leaders by some insane, demonic design.

"We as women always had to learn how to protect our men from white society," she said, remembering growing up in the fifties when a Black man, Mack Parker, was lynched in Mississippi after being accused of raping a white woman. She was fourteen when Emmett Till was murdered. Ladner reflexively hugged her body, leaned in closer to me as the memories induced an ache so palpable in her voice that I felt it too. Her voice fading to almost a whisper, she said, "When those men were killed, my fear was for my brothers, my uncles. I was a young girl scared for the men in my family. I remember having nightmares that someone would come and take all the men away. Today it's not the Klan in white sheets that's coming, it's more likely to be another Black male. Black women are still afraid for their men."

Each generation of Black mothers has hoped our sons would indeed become and always be the "Strong Men" poet Sterling Brown wrote of, who, undaunted and unbowed by racism, "keep coming, keep coming." And of our sons we eternally ask, how will they live, will they succeed? They must deal with myriad dangers, all while seeking always to know really who they are.

Our sons are Thomas Carrington, Ladner's pride and progeny, who would enter Syracuse University in the fall. They are my son, Michael, gangly, in the grip of a thunderous adolescence, baby-faced and grimacing. They are modern-day Dred Scotts, three fifths of a man, but now with an Uzi; they are football players, scholars, and would-be astronauts; they are William Horton, dubbed "Willie" in the racist corrupt ads of the 1988 Bush presidential campaign. They are Mike Tyson, National Merit Scholars, and an inner-city Black male infant, his prospects already curtailed.

They are not valued, nor listened to. They are not the problem but a symptom of a society in decay and decline, a society that has always used the Black man, the Black woman, the Black child, to symbolize its worst impulses, its throbbing underside. I know that the Black man has always been endangered. And if he is endangered, so, too, are his sister, his wife, and his mother.

Joyce Ladner and I represented the supposed realization of "equality" in the lives of contemporary African Americans. Yet our ascent into realms declared off-limits to our parents merely sharpened our ability to recognize the multitude of forms that institutional racism takes and its persistence. We were both women who saw whatever success we achieved in the white world as a tool to aid communities we were a part of no matter where we chose to live.

In several conversations over the weeks that followed my reading at Howard, Ladner and I talked about the complex equation that had produced this awful time. During one of our most wrenching dialogues, Ladner assessed the civil rights movement of which she was a part, saying, "There was a sense in which we wanted nice houses, decent schools, good neighborhoods so badly, and who could blame us, that we were willing to trade the good things in our community, the traditions, the beliefs, that were valuable in order to integrate." While Ladner was justifiably proud of the myriad social changes she had literally been part of creating, like many veterans of the civil rights movement with whom I had spoken, she now questioned the single-minded push for integration at the expense of protecting and enhancing Black businesses and the other institutions in the African-American community that had managed to serve us during segregation. Ladner's impassioned analysis represented not an attempt to mythologize an often unjust past; rather, her words symbolized a longing for a coherent present and future to give to our children.

At one point, she asked rhetorically, "What do we have to give our children now?" As we talked, I thought of the burgeoning and increasingly intense interest among middle-class African Americans in Afrocentric ideas, books, clothing, and styles. Men and women who worked in corporate America, calling institutions like Xerox and IBM "high-tech plantations," celebrated Kwanza, flocked to hear Nation of Islam head Minister Louis Farrakhan, gave their children African names. Yet hadn't we done this before in the sixties, sprouting naturals, wearing dashikis, fighting for Black studies, deigning and deciding to call ourselves "Black" with pride? And even in the 1920s, hadn't Marcus Garvey tapped into the best and brightest of our community to create a movement and an organization that were initially far-reaching, even though they are now erased from the books our children read? Weren't there "race men" and "race women" before? Yet each generation discovers, debates, dissects, and challenges the question of identity as if our race and our history were questionable propositions rather than undeniable facts.

Ladner concluded that this double consciousness, which we know both from the minutiae of our lives as well as from the pages of Du Bois's *The Souls of Black Folk*, is draining and sometimes killing our spirits. So often in the public and private discourse over integration, neither Blacks nor whites have assumed that African Americans brought anything of value to the process that would enhance white lives and world views. We came to the table as beggars, and even in three-piece suits and armed with honorary degrees, we are still scrambling for crumbs. We know that in our hearts. And so do our children.

And as the nation's economy is buffeted by such imperatives as "downsizing," increased computerization (which makes human hands obsolete), the influx of immigrants (who have taken over minimum-wage jobs that Black men once supported families on), and middle-class whites forced to take blue-collar jobs, where is there a job for my son? The trickle-down effect of misery fills street corners in the Black community with men who have never held a legitimate job. Work is available, but not enough for Black men who are unable to fill out a job application form even after graduating from high school, and who, because they are Black and male, instill fear and trembling in every white person in the company, from the receptionist to the head of personnel.

My son will know how to complete a job application. I will see to that. He will know how to stand with the right mixture of confidence and politeness as he enters an office suite, and he will know how to sell himself and his abilities articulately. But in an economy under siege and tunneling toward an ever-widening gap between rich and poor, employed and unemployed, what difference will that make? There will be fewer positions where a Black face will be tolerated. His confidence alone may instill more fear in the white man or woman who does the hiring and firing than a .38 pressed against their neck.

One evening, watching a Black politician on television—noting his smooth mastery of the jargon of intellectual and political discourse, his ease in the face of his interrogator, his regurgitation of the shallow doublespeak American politicians render so well—my husband, Joe, laughed, saying, "You know, I see now why whites are scared. If we turned off the picture, we'd think this guy was white. Hell, we can even beat them at that." With a shake of his head, he concluded, "They know if they level the playing field, it's over."

And so, my son may never inhabit a street corner as hustler or drug dealer, but he will have to be three times as good to get a job an "average" white man claims on the basis of genes alone. Affirmative action has put only a nick in the surface of that stony reality.

Considering the psychological circles we march in generation after generation, and the global and national economies we are victimized by, is it any wonder that in our communities the "drug boys" are major employers? We don't make the guns or import the dope, but despair and neglect motivate scarred, tremulous, even greedy hands to reach for crack vials. Yet who cares if 75 percent of the users are white? The drug boys introduce a level of fear, mayhem, and insecurity into the Black community that poisons relations between neighbors, lowers property values, and cheapens the meaning and essence of human life. Maybe it is true, as the popular slogan asserts, that we don't import the drugs or make the guns, but too many of our sons choose to reach for them.

Still, in the end and in the beginning, we can choose. Our sons and daughters must know that. Most of our sons do not sell drugs or brand their presence onto the surface of our memory through violence or mayhem. All of our sons need to recognize their lives as a memorial to the often graceful survival of African Americans who preceded them. Our sons must know that their lives belong to, and are claimed by, us all, and so they matter. Life has always mattered in the African-American community. Sometimes life—its potential, its bitter taste, its laughter ground into and alchemized by the ashes, its relentless hope—was all we had.

And so it is life that is the quest now. I want my son to grow up to be smart, productive, and content. But like every Black mother I know, I want my son, mostly, to live. White mothers insist, "I worry about my son too." And well they should. For while I seek to protect my son's life, any progressive, concerned white mother must strive to raise her son to resist and reject the legacy of his father. White mothers must raise their sons to welcome the necessary sharing of power, resources, and the world. White boys have to be taught to care whether my son lives or dies.

Michael is an Aquarius child, born on Valentine's Day like his maternal grandmother, who died seven years before his birth. At fifteen, he is five feet eight, nearly as tall as his father, towering six inches over me. Caramel-colored, he possesses his father's small ears and high forehead. Yet everyone has said I "spat him out," he looks so much like me. I see it too, in the cheeks, the curve of his lips. Thumbing through the photo album that charted his growth and mine, I see as well what is his alone. There is the smile, radiant, aggressive, always ready for the camera. There is no holding back, no shyness or hesitation. That is not me, always a bit uneasy before the camera, unsure whether to pose or be myself. Where I have resisted the camera, my son embraces it with unexpected mugging just before the flash, and with an ease that says, "Of course you want a picture of me."

One summer when Michael was six, I traveled to Belgium to visit friends I had made the year before during a trip to Senegal. Michael remained behind with a friend for three weeks and then flew alone to join me. When I met him at Charles de Gaulle Airport, the stewardess, grinning and shaking her head in amazement, told me, "He was seated next to a businessman from Chicago; they talked nonstop almost the whole flight."

Maybe it is his ability to talk that is my endowment. I play with, shape, and transform words on paper. Michael is enamored of their sound— their music and rhythm manifested through speech. He loves to tell jokes, make puns; and to my dismay, year after year in school he earned distinction as the class clown. At eight, he started reading the sports page daily and over dinner produced a new multisyllable word two or three times a week.

Burdened with talents and gifts, Michael drew well early and naturally, impressing the teachers in the Saturday afternoon classes at the

Corcoran Art School. He had a flair for cooking, was an agile, enthusiastic athlete, and, when interested, could master a subject quickly. The years before his adolescence now seem to have been an extended, auspicious gardening, the planting of the seed, the quiet, sometimes breathless tending, the praying for rain and hoping for sun. Then comes the breaking of the sod and soil. You wake up one morning and there it is, a seedling; there he is, an adult, a man.

That spring when I was searching for the souls, examining the lives, of young Black males, I was learning, often against my will, clumsily but insistently, to let go. And this feeling of letting my son go was as heady and intoxicating as holding him tight in my arms, tucked beneath my breast. We had spent our lives together traveling toward the moments that awaited us, moments when he would turn his back on my beliefs, reject and then reclaim a value I had told him to honor; years when he would discover, abuse, and master free will, revel in his independence, yet thank God, he could always come home if he had to.

What if he was like me in the end, restless, searching, remaking myself like clockwork every few years by a new set of fantasies and goals? What if he ever said what I said to my mother when I was nineteen, brazen and so emboldened by the gospel of Black Power that I stood before her, hands on hips, and prophesied, "We won't make any progress until your generation dies off."

In the car one afternoon after Michael and I left a bookstore where I had had a friendly conversation with the owner about my newest book, a conversation during which I playfully lapsed into a fake Southern accent, Michael observed moodily as we drove off, "Why do you do that?"

"Do what?"

"Act different around white people. You and Joe. I've seen you. It's like you're tomming with them or something, it's like with them you're somebody else." The words doused me with surprise, and an embarrassment I couldn't explain.

Angrily clutching the steering wheel tighter, I said, "Nobody's tomming. What you call tomming is being friendly, that's all."

"Oh sure." My son's voice was derisive, surprisingly bitter. "You both act like they're something special. You're just normal in a Black store or restaurant. You're not fake there, why?"

How was I to tell him that despite our dinner table conversations about African history, capital punishment, war in Europe, and economic crisis in America, of which he is routinely a part—conversations in which intelligence and compassion make the morass manageable—the world is not black and white but often fuzzy, muted, and out of focus. I didn't tell him that when Joe receives an inquiry about the rooms in the rental property we own, if the prospective tenant is a woman, Joe insists that I come to the interview with him. As his wife, I have a vested interest in this business matter too. But my presence, with a ring on the fourth finger of my left hand, also defuses some of what makes white women afraid and Black women suspicious, the fact that Joe is a Black man. Was I to tell Michael, that day in the car, that the world feared him? Maybe he already knew.

And so I said instead, "Michael, you don't know what you're talking about."

"Yes I do," he insisted defiantly.

"Being decent, even friendly, to whites isn't tomming, Michael, and I sure hope you don't think it is."

This anger, as fervent as a small brushfire beside me, represented my son's battle with the burden that his race has become in America. Perennially intractable, race as limit and as boundary had tied my son metaphorically in knots. This was how he would know one day that he was an adult. I had told him that he could be anything in a world where whites control everything political and material that matters. I had told him to respect himself, but my lectures about racism had perhaps instilled the suspicion that whites didn't deserve the respect he extended to himself. And, increasingly, I was lecturing him to be as careful around young boys who looked just like him as in the presence of white people who didn't. "Ambivalence" and "compromise" were words my son at fifteen could spell, perhaps even define. But they were words that had not yet tested his resolve or courage.

I was still dazed, flushed by the emotions Michael's accusation had unearthed. And as we turned onto our street, I heard him mutter again through clenched teeth, "When I grow up, I'll never be a tom."

I said nothing more, for I was letting go of him and it was messy and scary. He was letting go of me, and I wondered how that felt.

• • •

Once, we talked about everything. Now it seemed so hard. Was it because my son was a teenage Black male, and so, as a result, so much of what I felt compelled to say other than "I love you" was warning, caution, and critique? For Michael, the line of demarcation between child and adulthood was not a border but a precipice. There was so much to tell and so much he had to know, so little time and so few situations within which to frame the conversation.

Michael has the soul of a bear in winter, for at night, he sinks not merely into sleep but into a hibernation that defies alarm clocks, my screams up the stairs to get up, even sometimes the smell of pancakes in the kitchen. Meeting my teenaged son in the hall at seven in the morning was like running into a man with evil on his mind in a dark alley.

When he took up residence in the bathroom, his ever-deepening voice, resonating like a talking drum, filled the hallway with the latest hot rap lyrics, uttered so quickly in a battered staccato that they whizzed by like bullets ricocheting off the walls.

Allegedly awake, walking as slowly through the house as if each step had been choreographed for special effect, he would enter the kitchen wearing a shirt two sizes too big (he was in style), jeans, unlaced sneakers, a jacket inappropriate for the weather outside. Looking into the refrigerator (his favorite pastime), he'd grab a Sprite. "Not in this house," I'd say, lifting the soda from his hand and placing a glass of orange juice there instead. Apparently, breakfast was uncool, for it required five minutes of debate to get him to eat a slice of toast.

No time to talk now. I would hustle him out the door, fuming as I watched him walk as though he was on a picnic in the woods, not as though already late, toward the subway and school.

After school, when homework was done, he'd go outside, talk to boys on the block. I was cooking dinner once when he trooped in with two friends, Leonard and Calvin. No video games on school nights, no TV until after dinner, so the three boys sat in the living room trading baseball cards. While I moved between kitchen and dining room, it was Michael's voice I heard most as he regaled his two friends with anecdotes, statistics about players and games. With Michael's edgy yet playful laughter filling the house, he stood up before the other two to imitate a play, sprawled over the couch one minute, edged closer to Leonard the next to sell him a card. With his peers, he was natural and easy, and soon all three were laughing, joking. Michael was ringmaster of the event.

And yet he was comfortable being alone. Saturday afternoons he might spend in his room drawing, reading magazines, playing video games, and staunchly resist the call of friends to join them. As an only child, he learned to entertain himself, feeling perhaps that his thoughts possessed more integrity than the lure of tales others might weave. Of all the traits my son possesses, I admire most in him this independence. More than anything, I would wish for him a fierce loyalty to being who he is, who he wants to be—if need be, by himself.

Over dinner, finally there was time to talk—but not always of the most important things. Skillful mastery of the mundane, I had learned, was part of parenting too. With Joe teaching math three nights a week at Armstrong Adult Education Center, Michael and I could be alone. We talked about the news, school, family, friends. There were still times, even now, when we flashed back to an intimacy that I missed and he had not yet completely forsaken.

Many of our most memorable conversations took place in the car, driving to karate lessons or art classes, or on weekends when the three of us often headed to the mall for a movie. The car was where we talked about sex. I'd found a condom on the floor of Michael's bathroom the day before. The unused yellowish device, limp and harmless in my palm, symbolized all the "official" lectures about sex that Michael had endured. In the fifth grade, he brought home a form from school for me to sign giving permission for him to take the sex education class. I had bought a human anatomy book for children for him when he was five. In eighth grade, there were lectures on sexually transmitted diseases in health class. He was vaguely aware, I suspected, of the nuts and bolts and the mechanics of intercourse from all this, which equated the act with dissecting a frog or building a chair.

A few minutes into our drive—on this day, to the dentist—and after mentally sifting through the two dozen ways I had considered broaching the topic, I finally asked, "Where'd the condom come from?" I strove to balance nonchalance and concern, so as not to tip the always precarious balance we now seemed to maintain against full disclosure. Michael said he'd been given the condom during a lecture about AIDS prevention at the all-male after-school program he'd attended. During the lecture, the boys had practiced putting a condom on a banana. I was not certain, however, that this meant they would put it on themselves.

"Who'd you say gave the AIDS lecture?" I asked, stopping at a red light. I wondered if I sounded as wired to Michael as I did to myself.

"Some lady from the city health department."

"Oh." Uncomfortable pause. "You probably knew a lot of what she talked about, I guess, huh?" I said, wondering how much he really knew, realizing that we'd had a couple of brief conversations about sex, hit-or-miss, hit-and-run efforts, but nothing like the in-depth cozy dialogues with your child the manuals advise.

"I knew some of it." He shrugged, opening the glove compartment and reaching for a stick of gum. The sound of the gum wrapper being squashed by his fingers was the only sound in the car. I turned on the radio for support and asked, "What didn't you know?"

"Well, like about the different kind of condoms, the best ones to use, and how even when you do other stuff you can get AIDS."

"Other stuff?" I turned to look at Michael and he was gazing out his window, taking refuge in the sight of familiar streets.

"What other stuff? You mean like drug use?"

"I knew that," he said to the window, his voice nearly muffled.

"Well, what other stuff?"

"Like oral sex." Michael turned to face me now, his gaze gauging the effect of his words.

"Ooooooooohhhhhhh, oral sex," I said, as though I had never heard the words before in my life. Hoping to regain control, I said, "So much of what everyone tells you about sex, Michael, is clinical, and it's easy to lose the real meaning of it." I was back on solid ground, entrenched in the touchy-feely, slightly intellectual mode I handle best. But was he listening?

"I mean, what sex is really about is two people who respect and care for each other, and sex is an expression of that. You shouldn't, for example, have sex to prove anything. And there are so many emotions involved in having sex. Your body may feel ready, but you may not in fact be prepared, mentally I mean."

"A lot of my friends say they've had sex."

"A lot?"

"Sure. But I know they haven't. I can tell. When we're together, they say stuff like 'Yeah man, it was so good. She didn't want me to stop. I was killing her.' "

I sat imagining the young boys who entered our house to play video games and bicycle down to the mall talking like this. I nearly hit a pedestrian crossing the street.

"Does that make you want to have sex?"

"No. Not just because they did."

"Have you had sex?"

There, I've said it, I thought. Suddenly I felt lighter. I could even breathe again.

"No, I didn't have sex yet," he said calmly, but clearly anguished, angry, and embarrassed that I had asked.

"Well, don't rush into it. Don't do it with just anybody. You've got plenty of time."

"Okay, mom. Okay."

"Your body isn't something you share with just anybody. It's special, remember that."

"Okay, mom. Okay."

I was breathlessly issuing orders, pleading for sanity and safety. Relieved he hadn't had sex yet, yet still scared knowing one day he would, I added, "And when you do, use a condom."

"Okay, mom. Okay," he said gently, placing a hand on my arm as we arrived at our destination.

I turned to look at him, imagining an AIDS-emaciated face staring back at me, recalling the article I'd read chronicling the increase in AIDS among Black youth, citing it as a close second to homicides in some cities as the leading cause of death.

"If you don't ever want me to have sex, just say so." Michael grinned, brazenly sarcastic.

"Michael, I just want you to be careful," I told him, smiling as I attempted to be less grim. In the wake of this assurance, I thought, as I do every day, although I did not say it, "And I just want you to live."

Growing up in the Black community in the fifties in Washington, DC, I was part of the last generation that, across income and class lines, benefited from a pervasive network of family and kinship ties that effectively met the needs of mothers and children. In the summer, I visited my maternal grandmother, Molly Reid, in Greensboro, North Carolina. I recall my grandmother as a strict and often stern woman of silences, yet a woman who quickly garnered respect and attention when she chose to speak. These annual summer sojourns joined me to family; they fixed in my consciousness that I was a Golden, but also that I was a Reid.

Summer in Greensboro meant driving with my cousins Bunny and Fairdon and their mother, Aunt Janey, to visit her mother, "Ma Head," and eating fried chicken and apple pie or whatever Ma Head had on the stove while the two women talked on the front porch. Greensboro nights were tranquil, the darkness deep and solemn. My cousin Debra would come down from New York in the summer sometimes too, and we'd spend evenings chasing fireflies on Granny Reid's front lawn and imprison them in glass jars. In those summers, Greensboro, like all of the South, was rigidly segregated. Not for several more years would Southern Black college students assault institutional racism by sitting in at counters at Woolworth's or freedom riding their way on Greyhound and Trailways buses across the South. But for me as a Black child, the community of which I became a part for eight weeks each year was cocoon and buffer. The world beyond was racist and cruel, but my grandmother, my aunts, and my uncles all conspired to protect my cousins and me from the destruction that that world sharpened like a precise tool. And so Greensboro was my uncle Robie's effusive, effervescent laughter, his jokes and teasing. I did not know then that he was an alcoholic, I just loved the drenched gleam in his eye and his determination to handle anything that came along with a rakish, irresistible smile. When my uncle Robie died when I was a teenager, I used the memory of his laughter to defeat the terrible images of the alcoholism that had induced his death.

When I was very young, my mother's women friends often cared for me. And as I grew, I could call on a host of aunts and "play mothers," babysitters, birthday and graduation rememberers, and I'm-mad-at-Mama-so-I-need-to-talk-to-you-'cause-I-know-you-won't-tell-her-what-I-said confidantes.

In raising my son, however, I was unable to call on this kind of support. The education I had achieved endowed me with a mobility and appetites that loosened family ties. The Black family, mine and everyone else's, responding to the effects of integration and other social patterns, became less monolithic and communal.

But it was the deaths of my mother (of a cerebral hemorrhage when I was twenty-one) and my father (of a heart attack when I was twenty-two) that severed my sense of connectedness to human forces much larger than myself. Their nearly simultaneous demises abruptly launched me on a persistent, often relentless search for community, a sense of family, place, and roots.

My mother, Beatrice Lee Reid, was an extraordinary self-made, self-possessed woman who left Greensboro as part of the Great Black Migration of the late 1920s. She settled in Washington, DC, where, within a few years of her arrival, she had parlayed her modest earnings as a domestic worker, along with her penchant for winning at the "numbers game," into ownership of several boardinghouses.

I was born, much to my mother's surprise, when she was forty-two years old. I know now that I became a writer as much because I was an obedient child as because I could not help it. For it was my mother who had proudly watched me recite my poems in school pageants and plays, who had seen me at the age of ten mailing letters to the editor of the *Washington Post,* and who looked at me one afternoon across the kitchen table, where she stood rolling dough for biscuits, and said, "One day you're going to write a book."

I sat at the table, thumbing through a copy of *Little Women,* and was so stunned by my mother's declaration that I stammered out, "Oh, Mama, I couldn't ever do that." I told her this, I, the daughter who spent whole summer days in the attic reading as though her life depended on it, the daughter who walked past neighbors without speaking, neighbors she hadn't seen because at that moment a story was taking shape in her head. Ignoring my protests, my mother continued, embellishing what struck me then as an entirely fanciful proposition. "In fact, before it's all over, you probably will write more than one book," she said, smiling slyly, utterly pleased with herself and totally convinced of the certainty of her prediction.

I remember rising from the table, frightened and on edge. I fled the kitchen. My mother's words were so laden with the promise of power, the possibility of miracles, that I was literally trembling. I was twelve years old and my mother had baptized me. She could have told me I'd grow up to be someone no one would ever listen to. She told me instead that I was destined to write stories that would be hard to resist.

I had seen the house my mother was born in, once, during my annual pilgrimage to North Carolina. It was a weather-beaten, run-down shotgun shack, abandoned but still standing. The day my mother anointed me, however, we sat in a three-story house of twelve rooms, with oriental carpeting, a Zenith stereo, and gilt-edged mirrors. This was my mother's house. So I knew that a woman could become a "self-made man," could become who she needed and wanted to be. Still, I was astounded that day, thought my mother was crazy. Six years later, my mother gave me a subscription to the *New York Times* for my eighteenth birthday. I was entering American University in the fall and had talked about becoming a journalist. My mother wanted to initiate me into the language I would need to begin learning how to speak.

Because she gave birth to me in middle age, with each passing year my mother repeated like a litany, "I just want to live long enough to see you graduate from high school." Her large, always somehow mournful eyes appeared to miss me even as she spoke. When I graduated from Western High School, she amended her wish, saying, "I just want to live long enough to see you graduate from college." But she died in my junior year.

If my mother gave me the charge to write, it was my father who schooled me, rigorously, consciously, and unconsciously, in how to tell a story. My father, Francis Sherman Golden, was a very dark, intensely proud Black man. Partially named after the Union general who burned Atlanta during the Civil War, my father was abundantly, shamelessly charismatic, and he, like my mother and my son, was an Aquarius, loquacious and charming. My father spun for me tales of legendary figures from Black history. Hannibal, Cleopatra, and Frederick Douglass peopled my bedtime stories. My father was "Afrocentric" long before the term was coined. I learned from my father that a good story involves drama, conflict, change, growth. And years later, when I wrote about my parents, I envisioned them grand, heroic, larger than life, because in a sense they were, but also because with his voice, my father had etched for me the thrilling deeds of men and women who had transformed themselves and the lives of others. Estranged from his only son from a previous marriage, who was fifteen years older than I, my father raised me as though I were his favored son, taking me for rides in his taxicab as he ferried passengers all over the city, allowing me to follow him into gambling joints, sitting with me at night in the summer on the front stoop, or before the fireplace in winter, explaining politics, history, the entire world from his point of view. My father taught me that I was worth talking and listening to.

These were the parents I lost before they had a chance to watch me take on the world they promised me was and could and should be mine. These were the grandparents my son was denied.

What would my parents have thought when I fell in love with and married a young Nigerian architectural student and went to live in Lagos with him? As much as I wanted to create a family of my own, I wanted to somehow "recapture" my parents through marriage.

It was in Africa that I became a mother. I had married into a large Yoruba extended family whose members included my US-educated husband, Femi, and other similarly educated cousins and brothers and sisters, as well as family members who were barely literate. The Ajayis were a clan of strivers and upwardly mobile achievers. My husband's great-great-

great-grandfather had been a member of the royal court of a Yoruba king, and the entire family wore this genealogical inheritance like a cherished mantle.

My son was named, as custom allowed, by his grandmother: Akintunde Babatope—and also at my insistence, Michael. His first name means "The spirit of the father returns"; all the male names in the family carry "Akin" as a prefix. Babatope means "Praise be to God."

In my husband's culture, when a woman gave birth to a child, she gave up her name to be called "Mama [name of child]." It was a society in which fertility was worshiped, fecundity prized. So as a male, my son was not just welcomed but treasured. His gender bestowed honor and legitimacy on me, status on his father. My first child had also been a boy, but he had died three days after his premature birth at seven months. And so Michael held within him some part as well of the brother who had preceded him.

To celebrate the birth of our son, friends and family gave us monetary gifts totaling the equivalent of fifteen hundred dollars, and we held an elaborate naming ceremony which began with an old family friend acting as a priest addressing everyone gathered. He poured a libation, sprinkling gin onto the floor to honor the Ajayi ancestors, believed always to be present. My son was officially named as child of us all, belonging not just to his father, Femi, and to me but to all the Ajayi clan. Then the priest reached into several bowls placed on a nearby table and dabbed a bit of each ingredient (honey so life would be sweet, water so he would be great like the sea, salt so he would know that life is difficult) onto my son's tongue and mine and Femi's. After that, the bowls were passed around the room for all who had gathered to share. Later that evening, one of Femi's older brothers sat with me and celebrated the birth of my son by telling me the history of the Ajayi clan, acting as griot and charging me to tell the story to Akintunde one day.

I had wanted family, and it was family that I now had. But I had come to Nigeria a feminist and was confronted again and again by the regressive roles and treatment of women in my adopted country and what they portended for me and for my son. My mother-in-law, a feisty, quick-witted, intelligent woman, had worked long hours on her husband's rubber plantation, had sold foodstuffs in the market, and had borne three sons, two of whom she had helped send to study abroad. My sister-in-law helped my husband's brother work his way through school in London. She was a kind of human dynamo, running her household and her stall in the local market with breathtaking efficiency. Both these women and others like them were valued among the Yorubas because they worked hard and bore sons. Among the Yorubas, a woman was encouraged to be financially independent and to have a trade of her own.

But the journalism classes I taught at the University of Lagos were overwhelmingly male because it was considered a waste to send a girl to college. I knew that female children were still subjected to clitorectomies, a form of genital mutilation that no one I asked seemed willing or able to explain. Polygamy still flourished; it was respected and practiced widely. The few single Nigerian women I had met could not imagine themselves remaining single. One woman, a reporter for the country's most respected newspaper, told me, "There would be no place for me in my society as a single woman. I would not count, would not even exist in the minds of my family and friends."

Here was a country that was one of the largest, most populous, and most influential in Africa. My son was by birth a member of a tribe whose culture was deep, rich, and complex. We lived in a nation where the head of state was Black, where when I boarded a plane, the pilot was Black, and where all the women possessed my hue or some variation of it, as well as my broad hips. I saw some resonant, primal part of myself everywhere I looked. And I wanted this racial inheritance for my son.

But what was the inheritance really? Corruption in Nigeria was rampant, the oil wealth was being wasted, and I knew that a group of men could meet around a wood-paneled table in a bank in Luxembourg or London and, with a show of hands or their signatures on a piece of paper, cripple or completely destroy the economy of the country. Nigeria was large and populous, but like every country in the Third World, it was a nation of paupers. Its popular culture was schizoid, with young people who used bleaching creams on their skin and listened to American music, but visited juju men in moments of doubt. Half the population was still illiterate, and every attempt at democracy had been sabotaged by the military. What really was my son a part of? His heritage and inheritance here were as conflicted and bittersweet as the ones he would have had if born in America.

When I left my husband four years after I had arrived in Nigeria and a year after my son's birth, my departure had more to do with emotional incompatibility than with politics. Yet the expectations Femi and I brought to our union had been shaped by how we had seen men and women love one another in the cultures that had produced us. Culture and mythology are political; Nigeria taught me that.

Our separation and subsequent divorce were bitter and recriminatory; for me, they launched a long period of paranoia and fear that Femi would attempt to take Michael from me forever (a fear stoked by threats made repeatedly in the heat of anger and by my knowledge that in the Nigerian legal context, my son, no matter what a court in the United States said, "belonged" to his father). The decision to restrict Michael's access to his father and, for long periods of time, not to allow his father to know where we lived was a painful, difficult one. It was made, however, based on my knowledge of how Femi handled anger and frustration. He had never really trusted me with his deepest feelings. How could I trust him with our son?

Black fathers, actually and legendarily, have often been the psychological missing link in the African-American community. But I had known and loved my father; he was present in my life, a commanding, impossible-to-ignore influence, even after my mother left him. The specter of the shiftless can't-be-trusted-never-around-when-you-need-him-can't-or-won't-respect-or-protect-his-woman Black man harnesses and corrupts so many Black women's expectations of the men who are their fathers, husbands, lovers, friends, and sons.

And so the absence of my son's father in his life was not merely my own private tragedy. It was, in my eyes, a failure of community as well. For my divorce and my estrangement from my son's father pushed Michael and me closer to the starting line of a race we would have to run already crippled. After my parents' separation, I had witnessed how they forged forgiveness and respect from the remains of a passionate, difficult union. But I wanted to give my son the ideal family even though I knew it did not exist. I wanted him to have a father in his life, despite the statistics that informed me there were eighty-nine Black men for every one hundred Black women. Was that why I married an African? Maybe, I thought in my moments of greatest doubt, we can't escape history. But still, I tried.

Many days I did. I never would have imagined myself as a mother who willfully denied a child of mine his father.

The decision I made out of fear brought order to my life but little peace of mind. The prayers I mouthed each night, prayers that my son never heard, asked to know when I could reach out to a man I had once loved and now did not trust. When the answer came, it was my son who showed me the way.

· · ·

For five years after returning to the United States from Nigeria, Michael and I lived in Boston. I chose the city because I had developed a friendship with a woman from Boston while she was an exchange student studying at the University of Lagos. When I wrote her that I was returning to the States, she had agreed to help me get settled. After teaching for three years at the University of Lagos, I also thought I could easily find a teaching job in a city long considered an educational hub.

In the first years following my return, the contradictions of my life were vivid and almost insane. I was a writer whose words and thoughts thrust me into the public domain. Yet, quite frankly, in the years after my divorce, I became a woman who was hiding her son from his father. When I broke off communication with Femi, on several occasions Ajayi relatives resident in this country nearly found us. But they never quite did. This was my life, one I often felt doomed to live forever.

In Boston I was totally unprepared for the ethnic and racial balkanization I found. It was 1979, and the bruising, often violent battle over busing that had scarred the city's image still left smoke literally tingeing the air. White cab drivers refused to take me to my Roxbury apartment after dark. I was not welcome in "Southie," the Irish-Catholic enclave, the North End (Italians), or any part of Dorchester, where working-class whites predominated. For the first time in my life, as I searched for an apartment, I was openly, blatantly rebuffed because of my race.

The middle-class Blacks I met were insular and snobbish and too often tried to claim their ancestors came over on the Mayflower too. And yet the racial intolerance of the city was countered by a thriving arts and theater scene and some of the best museums in the country. This provided a partial salve for the sting of living in the most racially primitive city I had ever known. The weather was as hostile as many of the people I met, for winter arrived arctic and cruel in October and didn't depart until April or May.

My first job was teaching at Roxbury Community College, then a struggling stepchild of the state system of higher education. Housed back then in a former convent, its decrepit interior was one of leaky ceilings and small, overcrowded classrooms. But the student body—mostly older, often fully employed Africans, Caribbeans, African Americans, and Hispanics, with a few Asians and whites tossed into the stew—was hardworking and motivated. I learned as much from my students from Eritrea and Trinidad as I taught them. My colleagues were, like me, often disgruntled over our relatively low salaries and the dismal state of the building. But dedication to the students was never in short supply.

Michael was a year old when we moved to Boston, and I collected a bumper crop of day-care horror stories. There was the day-care provider I found from a list of city-approved centers for children under two. Each day when Michael was brought home at six o'clock, moments after she sped off, he gazed mournfully at me for several moments as though to be certain that we were alone, his small body tensed, clearly on guard, and then burst into a tantrum, crying, screaming, releasing a rush of pent-up rage. My even-tempered son had suddenly become a volatile neurotic, fighting and kicking me as I hustled him from the front door upstairs to our apartment.

After three days of scenes like this, I made an unscheduled visit to the center and found that the owner had regimented the children so intensely that the toddlers in her care possessed the arch obedience of small robots. Michael, I soon saw, was rebelling against this strict regimen the only way he knew how.

The very best, most nurturing day-care provider my son ever had was ironically denied a license by the city because the space in her basement where her center was set up was ten feet less than required. But she loved all the children in her charge with an enthusiastic, unabashedly maternal fervor, and the children made developmental progress that was so rapid it seemed designed as her reward. This woman kept my son during the day for a year. I knew she was unlicensed; she had told me that up front. But because she was so obviously gifted in her approach to children, I took a chance. Then one snowy January morning Michael and I arrived at her house and found the door locked. I checked with a neighbor, who told me that the woman had gone to Florida the night before, having been tipped off by a friend who worked for the city that she was to be inspected and would be fined heavily if caught with children in her care.

My son and I were entirely dependent on the patience, concern, and training of strangers. The "day-care question," and how it was solved, determined whether or not I could concentrate on my work. It controlled my son's emotional development and the peace of mind of us both. And because the welfare of children remains at the bottom of this nation's priorities, neither my income nor my class guaranteed competent care for Michael. Unfortunately, all children in America possess an equal opportunity to be poorly cared for, indifferently nurtured, exploited, or abused.

• • •

When I was hired as a full-time member of the Department of Mass Communication at Emerson College, the job boosted my salary as well as our lifestyle and possibilities. I moved from Roxbury to the South End, then in the throes of a frenetic process of gentrification. It was a neighborhood where Blacks, whites, gays, yuppies, and Hispanics all lived side by side but rarely mixed. I enrolled my son in an excellent private nursery school on Newbury Street owned by a Black woman.

Home for us was the Piano Factory, an artists' community where spacious studio apartments were carved out of a building that had once actually been a piano factory. This apartment building was everything the city outside its doors was not. Here was a community. My neighbors were photographers, dancers, painters, artists, struggling and successful. They hailed from New York City and Bolivia, Greece and Oakland. A small art gallery on the first floor displayed the work of resident visual artists; our children played in a grassy courtyard that had swings and a sandbox and an area where parents could sunbathe.

Maybe fate and circumstance had denied my son his father, but I determined I would give him everything else. Weekends we made trips to the city's impressive Children's Museum. I bought season tickets to a children's theater company. Our neighbors were artists like Paul Goodnight, whom my son saw fill canvases with rich, vibrant colors, life, and people. Michael listened to Paul and me talk, over incense and herbal tea, about art and Black folk and our artistic ambitions.

By the time Michael was six, he had petted baby llamas in the San Diego Zoo and spent two weeks in Puerto Rico, where I sat watching him build castles in the white, shimmering sand and thought that just watching him beneath a Caribbean sun was as much as I would ever want or need. And when I yearned for Africa, even as I feared a return to Nigeria, we spent three weeks in Senegal, where he climbed onto the cannons that guarded the slave castle on Gorée Island and where we made Jamaican friends who lived in New York and artist friends who lived in Belgium. And there were occasional holiday visits to Washington, DC, to visit family there.

Yet I often felt overwhelmed, lonely. I worried about what would happen to my son if I died, resented the fact that as a single parent I was always on call. I got no vacations, and despite numerous friends, I often felt there was no one with whom I could share the fatigue, frustrations, or triumphs inspired by the life I lived with my son. Michael had never really seen me loving his father. What could he possibly remember of his first year of life, a year that marked both his birth and the painful, tortured end of my marriage? More than once I prayed that he remembered nothing, since I could recall nothing from that year that I wanted to hold on to except his birth. While I had several close platonic friendships with men I'd met in Boston, lovers were few and far between. What, I wondered almost obsessively, was Michael learning about love from watching me?

The headlines during these years were a foreboding, shrieking backdrop for my personal anxieties and fears as they asked "Single Parents: How Bad for the Children?" or predicted "Single Parent, Double Trouble," "Woe Is One, Two Parents Are Better, It Seems." The demographics of the Black community had changed dramatically since my childhood, a period in which children born out of wedlock or even living with one parent were more easily absorbed into the fabric of the community by extended families who provided mother and child with emotional and material support. Parents were living longer, retiring later, and were too busy with hobbies and interests of their own to serve as built-in babysitters. The infusion of drugs and guns and the accompanying violence into the

Black community had created social problems so profound that even the strongest extended families were rendered incapable of answering the call of sons and daughters in need. Most of the women I knew raising children alone, even those who had parents to lend a hand, complained of feeling isolated, ignored, and misunderstood. And if you were a Black woman raising a male child, the Black community became a chorus of naysayers, assuming you were not up to the task of raising the kind of "man" the race needed to make progress, yet refusing to create institutional assistance that might make a difference. Everything and everybody, it seemed, conspired to convince me that I could not raise a boy who could become a healthy, productive adult. Men I dated entered my apartment and, watching Michael in a range of normal activities, critically concluded, like doctors examining a sick patient, "What he needs is a man in the house."

Yet I knew that generations of Black women had successfully raised male children who became decent, loving fathers and husbands and members of the community. And inevitably, along the way, the brightest of these boys sought out some coach, male teacher, deacon in the church, or uncle or friend for guidance and encouragement. Children know what they need and are often adept and skillful at finding it. In other cases, men stepped forward to help mothers mold the character of their sons.

I suffered moments of doubt and attacks of guilt as I raised my son, but most days I swallowed the guilt, pushed aside the doubts. I had neither time for them nor interest in allowing them to define my life. I plodded on, saying "yes" to me and my son even though the world gazed on skeptically, whispering "no" loud enough for me to hear.

For while I was raising a boy who would one day be a man, I was trying to raise a well-adjusted, loving, responsible human being whose yin and yang I wanted to balance. My son saw me get up and go to work every morning, felt me kiss him goodnight, and was in the presence, via my platonic friendships, of men who were capable and often accomplished. He got lectures on his history as an African American from me, watched my loyalty to my friends, bore my punishment when he deserved it, was served dinner every night at six, and was bought encyclopedias and video games.

Still, how would Michael judge, and remember, me? How would he see me in memory, as I tried to be mother and father too? As a Black woman raising my son alone, did I sometimes let him become for me the "good man" I feared I might never find? I was not supposed to have come this far; he was not supposed to have turned out so well. Because we were African American, pathology and defeat were assumed to be our mother/son legacy. How could I raise Michael against the odds, and with laughter and gentleness? In a world where whites assumed whiteness equaled the universal human experience, I had to teach my son that his race was not a crucible and that all the people whiteness tried to render invisible possessed beauty he must see, wisdom he should learn. And as his mother and on some days father too, I was afraid for him and for myself. I was lonely and confused. Yet the need to keep my son fed, clothed, and loved propelled me, stoked ambition, satisfied hunger.

The "rap" against Black mothers is that we spoil our sons and raise our daughters. Denied by past and current racism, lacking competent adult partners, we shower our sons with the affection we hunger for, overinvest ourselves emotionally in their dreams, all to live vicariously through them. This is the charge. But in a racist, patriarchal society, how else, it might be asked in response, are some Black women to be realized if not through sons—sons who even under siege can in full flower ascend in ways still denied to women? Mothers in cultures around the globe, not just in Black communities in Chicago or Detroit, invest their own denied ambitions in their sons. Only in a world where women's goals are not stunted will this equation no longer persist. Mothers often see fragile, ephemeral hope when they look at their daughters; they see rock-solid possibilities when they gaze at their sons.

But I didn't spoil Michael; I raised him, knowing it was just the two of us, envisioning him as a resource for his family, his people, and his planet. I raised my son fearing I was not enough, imagining neurosis, psychosis, incubating within his spirit because of his absent father, the father I chose to leave. I carried all this, and remnants of it still snag projections and plans. Black mothers have transformed the shouldering of pain and responsibility and regret into a cryptic art form.

I despised the term "single parent," for I knew that no one ever really raises a child alone. The challenge I faced as my son grew was to build a surrogate family that would meet our need for community and connections. The search and need for family were part of the reason I had married Femi. This time I turned to the church.

Through a friend who lived in the Piano Factory, I began attending a small, racially mixed Baptist church in the neighborhood. The intimate congregation numbered only a hundred members. I was assigned to a "small group" of eight members who initiated me into the church and introduced me to other members with whom I engaged in weekly Bible study. There was no official or unofficial dress code at this church, and the God who prevailed here accepted congregants in blue jeans, dreadlocks, shorts, or three-piece suits. Following the service, everyone gathered for dinner in the church basement and it was not uncommon for a homeless man or woman to break bread with us.

During each service, there was a period where congregants could simply stand to share problems for which they sought prayer or to reveal good news. Much of the most vibrant spiritual energy in this church flowed from the membership to the pastor and mutually among the congregants. In the placement of the pulpit (centered and on the same level as the pews), in its expressed and acted-upon spirit, the church deconstructed the minister as all-knowing patriarch and invested the membership with a sense of their own significant abilities to heal and to teach.

I became close friends with a white couple, Rudy and Sara Maxwell, who were leaders of my assigned "small group." As a child, Sara had lived with her missionary parents in Colombia. She spoke fluent Spanish and was active in the church's outreach programs to the neighborhood's growing Hispanic community. Her husband, Rudy, was quiet, gentle, and scholarly. With Rudy and Sara, I discussed and bemoaned US involvement in El Salvador and the attempts to undermine the Nicaraguan Sandinista government. Michael and I drove with them and their two children, Joel and Laura, to view the spectacular New England fall foliage, and when I went into the hospital for minor surgery, Michael stayed with Sara and Rudy, as he did when I traveled to do a reading at a college. If Rudy and Sara needed to get away for the weekend, Laura and Joel stayed with Michael and me. For the last three years I lived in Boston, this network of friends and friendships became the surrogate family that I had known my son and I needed, that we could not in fact have lived successfully without.

I fashioned a multicultural, interracial world for Michael to be cared for and sheltered by. This church family worked in tandem with my actual family and friends, made up of people like an old friend of my mother's whom I had always called "Aunt" Bert. Thelbert Hines had come to Washington, DC, from Wilson, North Carolina, in the same era during which my mother left Greensboro. She at one time had managed one of my mother's rooming houses and had witnessed her marriage to and separation from my father. She celebrated my mother's gambling wins with her, helped her grieve over financial and emotional losses. When my mother died, I asked Aunt Bert if I could consider her my surrogate mother, and she said, "Of course, dear, you know you can." I did not need, however, to ask her to be grandmother to Michael. Each Valentine's Day, a birthday card arrived in the mail for my son with a money gift inside. Christmas gifts she allowed Michael to choose, visiting us and turning a shopping trip into a family reunion. But most important, Aunt Bert called regularly, frequently. She did not require a season or a holiday to drop us a line or give us a call to make sure we were okay. This woman represented the spirit of extended family and extended love that had enabled Blacks to survive, 'buked and scorned but with pride.

• • •

My task as a Black parent was to enable my son to positively assert and define himself in a society that had perfected diminishment of who and what he really was. But the group morality of my community and the external realities imposed upon us required that Michael become culturally flexible and open. I wanted him to meet whites and Hispanics and Asians and people of all races whom he could befriend and respect, to give him a sense of the breadth of human possibility. I also wanted him to recognize early on that whether or not he was "equal" to anyone else was a question that was offensive, superfluous, and irrelevant.

Watching Rudy read stories to Laura and Joel or talk with Sara, Michael witnessed a family different from the one he and I comprised. He saw that "family" often defied singular definition. And I watched my son, content and secure in the expanded domestic realm we—strangers, friends, parents—had created. Michael simply liked and trusted the Maxwell clan. With my own family miles away in other cities, they served as an immediate, present source of support for us both. The intense mutual dependence of mother and child in one-parent homes can breed in children anxiety and fear, often unexpressed, about the safety, future, and health of the parent. If I worried about what would happen to Michael if I died, I know that he was haunted as well by the same fear.

The Maxwells allowed Michael to claim a larger, more resilient sense of what he was connected to, what he could count on, and who would be there for him when I could not be. I measured Michael's satisfaction in the ease with which he climbed on Rudy's lap for a story, and in the manner in which Laura and Joel made room for Michael in the circle of their father's affection. I saw it manifested in the generosity with which my son shared our home with his young friends. I became friends as well with Janiece, a Black woman who was a member of our "small group." She was divorced, and her former husband often took Michael along on Saturday outings with him and their son, Jason. I knew I was lucky, as well as blessed, in the wondrous magnanimity with which we as parents salvaged and inspired the best that we possessed for the sake of our children.

In our friendship, Sara and I were spiritual and emotional confidantes. She had been married for a decade and had been a full-time wife and mother. She admired my career and my various journeys. I was attracted to her deep religious faith and her generosity, which led her to work in the church co-op and engage in numerous community projects that cared for the elderly, the illiterate, and the poor. Sara possessed a political savvy that most people thought was simply charm but that constantly intrigued me as I watched it unfold, whether in her handling of church matters or in dealing with social service agencies for a newly arrived immigrant.

One afternoon as we sat in her apartment sipping tea, Sara observed suddenly, "You know, I really admire how well you handle being a single parent."

"How well?" I asked, genuinely surprised.

"Yes, I mean I just don't know if I could do it, if something happened to Rudy," she said, hugging a throw pillow as she sat on the sofa, as if to shield herself from the implications of the thought.

"You'd do it if you had to."

"Yes, I guess you're right, but I just don't think I'd do it as well as you."

Reflexively, I wondered if Sara thought that as a Black woman, I was more prepared genetically, sociologically perhaps, to raise a child alone than she. I had no secret weapon, no special strengths as I raised Michael, acting as mother/father/breadwinner. And the support that she and Rudy provided had plugged up the holes in my steadfast but often vulnerable resolve. Yet in Sara's words I heard the pernicious "other side" of the mythology that hounded Black single mothers, a belief rooted in the stubborn remnants of the matriarchal myth.

Was this a genuine compliment, I wondered, one I was too insecure to accept gracefully, or did Sara harbor racial stereotypes that can cling even to a consciousness as independent and inclusive as hers? She was resilient, confident. I had witnessed her chair board meetings at church and rock Joel to sleep at night. Why would she question her ability to raise her children without a husband in the house? For the same reasons I wrestled with that question every day.

My insecurities were constantly fed and stoked by the larger society as well as my own community. Citing prisons filled to bursting with Black men, the exploding rates of homicide and teenage pregnancy, Blacks employing the time-honored tactic of female scapegoating argued that I could not accomplish this task. Conversely, whites felt that my history, my inherent psychological makeup, prepared me eminently, virtually by right, to shoulder this weight—and even more—alone. Was I incompetent or Amazon? I knew the answer, but its complexity discouraged anyone from hearing it, even when I gathered the courage to speak its name.

Remembering those years, I am awed by my hunger to have—by the determination I marshaled to invent—a family and a community for my son. When I think of the Black youth in crisis in our community, endangered by racism, incompetent parents, and dangerous home environments, I often have fantasies of forming a brigade of concerned men and women. We would simply walk into homes where our children were at risk, claim them in the name of the future, bundle them up, and take them into the many homes we have where love flourishes and order exists. In this vision, we are knocking on doors and defeating ignorance, hostility, even threats of violence, with the power of love for our children. Our righteous presence silences verbal threats, forces guns to slide from palms, empty their cartridges, and then disintegrate. We are on time. We are taking care of business. We are not waiting for things to get worse. We are loving our children and their lives completely, right now.

· · ·

In the fall of 1983, I quit my job at Emerson College. I was in the grip of a depression, manifested by a severe case of teacher burnout. After eight years in the academy, in the past year I had found myself fleeing the eager faces of my students at the end of each class. Many mornings I overslept, preferring to stay in bed rather than take on another day. Many afternoons I walked down Tremont Street toward the Piano Factory choking on a backlog of barely suppressed tears. I yearned for some grand, shattering experience that would shake up the predictability of my life. My always fragile tolerance for Boston's tribalistic racial atmosphere was demolished when a Black man was run over by a subway train after being chased by a bat-wielding group of white men attempting to drive him out of their neighborhood, one of a series of brutal attacks by whites against Blacks that year which resulted in the death or maiming of the victim. I wanted Michael to grow up in a city where he could see Blacks in positions of power and authority. Even pseudo power (the only kind we really had) was better, I reasoned, than what he witnessed in Boston. The city had become an intolerable place for me as a Black woman to raise my son.

It was this desire to challenge and test myself, this willingness to delve into the unknown, this penchant for creating myself over and over again, that had given the life I lived with Michael its energy, drama, and wealth. When we traveled from city to city and country to country, we were pilgrims. Each time we packed our bags, I was informing my son that the world was his. And so, I quit a good job, moved out of a spacious brick-walled, hardwood-floored apartment, and said goodbye to our surrogate family and a host of friends—this time, to go home.

Since leaving Washington after graduating from college, I had avoided even the thought of returning there to live. For me, the city was possessed by the ghosts of the mother and father who had not just died but had, I felt, deserted me. But Washington was politically and racially more hospitable than Boston, I had relatives there, and while I would have to start over again, by this point in my life, that thought no longer frightened me, and some days I wondered if it ever really had.

A year after my return "home," I met Philip, a photographer and graphic artist. Moody, aesthetic, he told me once he had considered becoming a priest. He, too, had traveled and lived in Africa, and like me, he was searching for union with a spirit and a soul that echoed his own. Six months after we met, we began living together. We talked of marriage but never went through with it. His mother had died of cancer when he was ten. Sometimes, memories of his childhood in the projects on welfare, of being shuttled during his mother's illness and after her death between the homes of relatives who considered him a burden, of not knowing who his father was, overwhelmed him and he burrowed within himself, silent and withdrawn for days at a time.

Yet in his relationship with Michael, Philip consistently found a way to tunnel a path out of his own private darkness. He, who had never known his own father, became a loving and loved, discipline-demanding, communicative, nurturing father figure to Michael. Philip taught my son karate, spent hours on Saturday afternoons with him in the video arcade, watched Sunday afternoon Redskins games with him, supervised his homework, and by his presence provided my son with a living model of maleness to imitate and respect. And Philip taught me, for Michael's sake, to loosen my maternal grip on the son I loved more than my own life.

In our relationship, however, Philip was less assured, and our affair was as tumultuous as his relationship with Michael was steady. We both desperately wanted to forge ties that would bind. But in the end, Philip possessed too many demons he could not overcome. His insecurities fed and stoked mine. I often felt imprisoned by a cauldron of feelings that were passionate, extreme, mercurial. Mostly, loving Philip, I felt out of control.

Sometime after the first year of our affair, I knew it had to end. But Philip's talent with Michael, his absolute loyalty to and concern for my son, always gave me pause. Maybe, just maybe, we can make this work, I told myself over and over, the words sounding more hollow, more false each time. I repeated them like a weary mantra. Since I was a parent, my life unfolded before my son's eyes on an invisible stage. Every day he had a front-row seat. Soon I was willing to admit that whatever confidence

Philip instilled in my son through his affection for him was undercut by the conflicts Michael witnessed between Philip and me.

How well did he really love my son, I wondered, if he loved me so ineptly? How would Michael learn to be open with a woman as he watched me unsuccessfully chip away at the boulder of silence that Philip, like Femi, too often imposed? I shuddered at the thought that in my relationship with Philip, I was informing Michael that love was some restless, quake-and-thunder-filled landscape, that I was teaching him the lesson I had learned from my parents: that real love hurts, a lesson it took me twenty years to defeat and deny.

I spent nearly nine months deciding what to do, a period of backsliding, second-guessing my most trusted instincts, and being racked with guilt about the impact of my decision (whichever one I chose) on Michael. Then one day, two years after Philip moved in, I woke up one morning and, by noon, told him he had to leave. He vigorously resisted my request, countering my assertion that whatever we once had was over with promises I had heard before. But I was not in the throes of a "mood," as he chose to believe, one I could be cajoled or talked out of. I wanted my life back. I was ready to live without Philip, realized, in fact, that if peace was to inhabit the home I was making for my son, Philip would have to leave.

I chose, as I had when I left Femi, to place my emotional health and the needs of my son on an equal footing. My decision was not simply a matter of putting me first. I was raised by a mother who walked away from three husbands when the love they offered degenerated into the confining or the destructive. And so I knew that in leaving Philip, I would, once I got past the pain, find an equilibrium, a confidence that my son needed in his mother much more than he required a "man in the house." I would hurt. Michael would too. But I could hold on to him, urge him to hold on to me and cling to the strengths that resided within himself, as we stumbled through it all.

• • •

I heard the laughter of the neighborhood children playing outside, heard a bat thunder against a ball, hoping, as I wrote another line, that no windows were broken. And I sat listening, as I often did, for Michael's voice. I had written five pages nonstop, and tossing the pen aside to rest my aching fingers, I looked up and saw my son standing in the doorway of my bedroom.

At eleven, he was tall. That evening, however, he stood with his shoulders hunched in despair and brooding defeat. The lips that smiled so easily and so often were pursed, a grim, unforgiving line etched across his face. His eyes were so vacant, there was no way to even guess what thoughts plagued him at that moment. The effect Philip's departure had on Michael introduced me to a side of my son I had simply never seen before.

The reasoned explanations for my breakup with Philip, which I had practiced and then delivered like a transparent political speech, had only increased Michael's grief and anger. Philip was the only father figure my son had ever known intimately. And the day Michael came home from school to find all of Philip's clothes removed from the closets and his photos stripped from the walls, my son locked the door to his room and refused to come out until the next morning.

A few days later when Michael was running late for school, I entered his room and found him standing before his chest of drawers gripping the top of the bureau, his teeth clenched, his eyes red from crying. I touched his shoulder and he flinched, turning to look at me, his look slicing me into tiny pieces. When I asked what was wrong, he whispered, "I feel so angry. I'm so mad. I want to kill somebody."

I held him, hugged him close, but he refused to cry in my arms and I felt him against me brittle, sealed shut.

That spring evening, however, several months after Philip had left, I braved a tiny smile, patted a spot on the bed beside me, and asked, "What's wrong?"

Dropping his catcher's mitt on the floor, Michael sat on the bed beside me.

"Nothing," he said, shrugging.

"Nothing? I don't believe that."

Michael sat picking his fingernails, dirt-filled from play, hedging, gathering courage. Frightened by the depth of Michael's grief over Philip's departure, unable alone to help him sort through and master his conflicted emotions, I had arranged for him to see a counselor at Howard University, Audrey Chapman, a family therapist. She had told me how difficult it would be for Michael to reveal his pain. As I was the only parent he had, he feared that if he angered me, he might lose everything. But sitting beside my son at that moment, I did not feel like the omnipotent controller of his life that to his young eyes and in his young mind I was. I sat beside him feeling, as I imagined he felt then, small, tremulous, and afraid.

"What's that?" he asked, pointing to a diary I had been writing in.

"A journal I'm keeping."

"About what?"

"About you and me."

"And Philip?"

"And Philip."

"Who is my family besides you?" he asked finally, slowly, carefully, after poking at the beginnings of a hole in his jeans and staring at his hands and daring a quick look at me from the corner of his eyes, a look that retreated so fast, maybe I didn't see it at all.

"What do you mean? You know who your family is."

"All the other kids have cousins and stuff. Edward told me he's going to a family reunion next week. Where's my family?" he asked angrily, now looking at me head-on.

"You want cousins?" I asked, thinking fast. "I've got cousins in North Carolina and they've got kids, so that means you've got cousins too."

"How come we never see them?"

"We're just not that close."

"How come?"

"No reason. We just aren't."

"How will I ever see them?"

"Well, I'll call them, I'll let them know that we want to visit them."

"When?"

"Soon."

I had mastered the art of burning bridges. Now my son was demanding that I build some instead, and lead him across them into the arms of people at whom he could look and see a facial feature, watch a walk, hear a laugh that he would recognize because blood made it his too. That evening I heard what my son had asked. I heard what he did not say. Michael had chosen to ask me for his father by asking for his family. Two or three times a year I had practiced a ritual with my son. We would spend an evening going through photos of his father, pictures that captured the woman I had been, the life I had lived in Nigeria. My son knew who his father was, and I told him again and again rationally, precisely, that his father was a good man who loved him and whom I had loved, but that because of problems I could not solve, I had had to leave him.

Children possess an emotional radar their parents never suspect. Michael had to have sensed the tenseness, the stilted quality that invaded my voice when I spoke of his father and that belied the intent of every word. And when he asked, as he sometimes did, when he would see his father and I answered too quickly, brusquely at times, "One day," I know now how impossible and even cruel that must have sounded to his young ears. For I loomed like a genie over the landscape of his life, in full possession of the power, he thought, to easily retrieve his father if I wanted to. He could not imagine my fear of losing him, the fear I felt as I imagined opening our lives up to Femi once again.

I had used my fear for Michael's safety to justify denying Femi access to his son. But wasn't my arbitrary separation of father and son as cruel as Femi's threats to take Michael from me? Fear had inspired me to interrupt and possibly stall the dynamic of healing that might have arrived sooner than I thought. I dreaded seeing Femi as much because of the guilt I felt as because I imagined recrimination and anger as his only possible responses to me. In my anguished fantasies, I never once assumed that Femi would be capable of rejoicing in reunion with his son rather than castigating me.

Audrey Chapman told me of the sessions where Michael talked about Philip, how much he missed him, how angry he was at me for making him leave. She told me that finally in the third session, Michael had cried, wept long and hard for the father figure he had lost and the father he did not know. For Philip's love, his presence in our life, and his leaving had become a catalyst that disturbed the dormant wound of my son's absent, unknown father. Some sessions, she asked Michael to draw pictures of Nigeria and his father, and he used the crayons and pencils to shape tentative yet hopeful sketches that they discussed and analyzed. But Michael never once mentioned them to me.

Near the end of Michael's sessions with Chapman, she told me that some issues had surfaced in their conversations which she thought I should be aware of. And, she said, she felt that Michael should tell me face-to-face what these "issues" were. "Children are deeply affected by the decisions their parents make," she said, trying to calm the apprehension she saw clearly in the worried expression on my face. "Yet rarely are they permitted to honestly and openly tell parents how they feel, how they've been affected by those choices." I loved my son, but even for me, a parent who had forged often unconventional answers to the challenges we faced, the prospect of submitting to an assessment of my life rendered by Michael terrified me.

The day of the joint session arrived, after an anxious week of waiting and wondering what Michael was going to say. Chapman began the session by talking for several minutes about the importance of what was going to take place and the significance of Michael's feelings. Then Michael, without an instant of hesitation (although I had expected a few moments' reprieve), turned and asked, "Mom, why'd you stay with Philip all that time?" I felt myself crumbling beneath his patient gaze and the confusion I heard in his voice.

"Well," I began slowly, stalling for time, "I loved him." I sat wondering how bad this was going to get. Yet even as I told him this, the words "I loved him" sounded like a hurriedly conceived excuse for a major crime.

"But he made you feel bad. I could tell."

"He wasn't a very happy person," I said lamely, the muddy tapestry of my relationship with Philip slowly rising before my mind's eye.

"But he made you feel unhappy." So, I hadn't been able to hide anything, I thought, amazed at and grateful for the level of my son's empathy.

"I wanted him to stay because I knew he cared for you. You cared for him." At twelve, without the guidance of a counselor schooled in psychology, I had asked my mother the same questions about my father. I had found it unfathomable that she could not simply walk away from a man who so often made her miserable. When she told me she remained with my father in part because of his love for me, the conflicts and contradictions of the answer, its heartfelt and heartbreaking demands, were more than my adolescent mind could comprehend. Now I was a woman who had walked in my mother's shoes. I knew some part of what my son felt at that moment.

"Yeah, I liked him a lot. It's just that it made me feel sad when he made you get upset or angry."

"Why didn't you say something?"

Michael gazed at Audrey Chapman, then told me, "I wanted to help, to make you feel better. Mom, I didn't know how."

The scheduled forty-five minutes turned into an hour and a half as Michael confessed that his loyalty to me had competed with what he felt for Philip. He had wanted Philip to stay. But seeing my misery, he wanted him to leave. And his inability to intervene in the skirmishes that flared between Philip and me increased his sense of helplessness and his lack of faith in us both.

How do I assess what my son lost in those years without his father? How dare I? Femi's need to control by instilling fear, my repudiation of the past through possession of our son, had left us all bereft, stripped of vital connections. I hail myself as a writer, yet even with words I am afraid to attempt a precise computation of the toll. In the end, I know only that I was a mother who loved her child. In the end, I did not make the "right" choice as much as I made the choice I could live with.

And yet, along the way, my son came to his own conclusions. One evening we sat reading together. I frequently chose to explore a book with Michael, with each of us alternately reading passages and discussing the text. He was twelve then, and we were reading the autobiography of the athlete Bo Jackson. In the book, Bo spoke candidly of growing up poor and of the anger he had often felt and directed at his mother. Bo recounted numerous incidents of youthful antisocial behavior, spawned, he felt, by his resentment of his absent father and his mother's inability to provide adequately for her children. But it was clear that what angered Bo most was the precariousness, the meagerness of his life, the constant material need. His anger was so forcefully stated that I paused in my reading to ask Michael if in growing up with only one parent, he had ever felt similar emotions.

His answer was astonishingly quick and confident. "No," he told me with a vehement shake of his head. "You've done everything a man could do." My son was judging my effectiveness as a parent. He was also disputing the myth that love alone is enough. Children need to see their parents as capable of providing for them. Watching parents do this, children learn that the world is a fair and reasonable sphere for them to enter, one that they can trust.

• • •

As I had promised Michael, I contacted my cousins, and, several months later, we journeyed to Greensboro for a wonderful reunion. And a week after the talk in my bedroom, I wrote his father. I had decided to write Femi once Audrey Chapman revealed to me what was coming out in the sessions with her. But it required several weeks of prayer, meditation, and rejecting the advice of friends who cautioned, "You've ensured your son's safety all these years, why risk it now?" before I sat down one evening and wrote a two-paragraph letter to my former husband.

I was exhausted by the years of fear. And I was more afraid of my son never forgiving me if I denied him his father than of any attempt his father might make to take him from me. I was a risk taker. And I computed with my heart and my head that Michael and I had nothing to lose and everything to gain by reaching out to his father now.

In this I was following the script my mother had written for me. Despite my father's numerous affairs and the ruthless manner in which he squandered her financial resources, my mother insisted that I respect and love my father. "He's the only father you've got," she'd tell me. "And that means you have to love him." Whatever bitterness she felt, she refused to pass it on to me. Because I grew up loving "the only father I had," it was imperative that I give my son his father too.

Six weeks after I wrote Femi, I received a response. The envelope contained a letter for me and one for Michael. The tone of the letter was grateful, conciliatory, and without a trace of the recrimination I had feared. I raced upstairs with the letter when I pulled it from the mailbox, shouting for Michael as I entered the apartment. I had told him I had written his father but had been careful to caution him that I could not predict when we would hear from him, or even if he would write back. My son and I sat that afternoon reading first his letter, then the one Femi had sent to me, over and over. Michael was smiling for the first time in months as he held his letter. After a while he took it into his room and lay on his bed reading it and holding it, and then placed it beside his plate at dinner.

In the months that followed, Femi and I wrote frequently. I sent him photos of Michael. He sent us pictures of himself. The morning we made our first call to Lagos to speak with Femi, I woke Michael up at five in the morning (because of the time difference) to speak with his father in his office. The first call was stilted, a bit awkward for us all. Michael sat on the edge of his bed, drowsy, his eyes filled with sleep, yet smiling and satisfied as his father plied him with questions about school, his friends, his hobbies, and his ambitions. And soon Femi's brother Bade, who lived in Brooklyn, became Femi's stand-in, calling frequently, updating Michael and me on news of the family in Nigeria.

Six months after I received Femi's letter, Michael and I spent a weekend with my cousin Debra and her husband and young son in Edison, New Jersey. My cousin was a vice president at one of the largest banks in New York City. She had enthusiastically supported the idea of my contacting Femi. A year before I left Nigeria, Debra had visited me. She liked and respected Femi, yet was part of a small but important circle of support I had relied on during the days and months when I first returned to the United States. We had a long talk that weekend about Michael spending more time with her family so that her husband Ed could take him fishing on his boat and play a more pronounced "big uncle" role. Debra's relationship with her father, my mother's brother, had been sometimes distant and sporadic in the years before his death, yet her memories of him were generous and affectionate. And so Debra knew how much Michael needed a "congregation" of fathers, formal and informal, to surround him.

Sunday morning of that weekend, Michael and I took the train from my cousin's house into New York and met Bade at Penn Station. Femi's father was polygamous, and Bade and Femi were not born of the same mother. Yet they were bound by the blood of their father and so their brotherhood was considered complete. Always the family mediator, Bade was a gentle man whose warmth had made him one of my favorite Ajayis when we first met in Nigeria.

Bade was accompanied by his wife, Cecilia, and their three children. For Bade, my son was Akintunde, not Michael, and he embraced him, assuring him that even during the years of estrangement, he had never been forgotten. Cecilia and I chatted on the subway to Brooklyn, and Bade plied Michael with questions and then sat silent for long moments, holding Michael's hand, marveling at the sight of him. In Bade's apartment, Michael gave his young cousins Akin, Lola, and Fola the video games I had brought for them and helped them improve their Nintendo skills. After a traditional dinner of chicken and jollof rice, Bade showed Michael a large black-and-white photo of his great-great-great-grandfather. In the photo, the man was draped in royal robes and sat flanked by several courtiers. Bade told Michael a story of service by their royal ancestor to a king, of Ajayi bravery in war, fidelity in marriage, of Ajayi children born generation after generation, of Ajayi migrations from the midsection of the country to the western coast. Michael sat rapt, quiet, blessed. And then Bade gave Michael a picture of Femi's father dressed in formal robes and speaking into a microphone, obviously addressing a crowd. He was tall, imposing, with the face of a leader, which, as a chief and owner of hundreds of acres of land, he was in his community.

Then there was a call to Nigeria so that Michael could speak with Bade's sister. Bade reached his sister Folake, who used to be a seamstress in their hometown of Ado Ekiti but who now was a contractor selling everything from cement to foodstuffs. She and I talked, her greeting to me ecstatic, studded with short prayers thanking God that she was hearing my voice. Then she spoke with Michael. It did not matter that my son had no memory of this woman who knew him three days after his birth. What mattered was that he, like she, was an Ajayi, and her lavish, enthusiastic greeting had been saved for this moment. That Sunday the meaning of my son's name, "the spirit of the father returns," was never more true. Bade walked us to the subway that evening, and we promised to stay in touch, a promise we both kept.

On the train back to Washington, Michael was quiet and reflective, and at one point asked, "If my great-great-great-grandfather was a king, what does that make me?" I could feel how energized and satisfied he was by this day. "I guess that makes you a prince," I said, smiling, and squeezed his hand.

• • •

Back in Washington, as Michael moved closer to adolescence, I fashioned a bulwark of concerned adults to surround and help guide him. I applied for a Big Brother for him, and he was partnered with a young Black investment banker named Loren Tate. Loren not only took Michael to the requisite baseball and basketball games but took him to his job one day to spend a few hours watching him work; and even when the demands of his work did not allow him to see Michael as often as he preferred, he made up for that with telephone conversations. Watching Loren with my son, I learned as I had with Philip that while fathers may not be required in the lives of young boys, capable, caring men are. And I knew, too, that all the "male role models" in the world could not reach a boy unless he had been consistently, purposely loved and cared for, unless he had already been taught and was prepared to trust himself and others.

Missing the emotional support that Philip had offered, I formed a single parents' group. I put the word out through friends and placed an ad in the city paper, and soon there were seven of us, six women and one man, meeting once a month. We were divorced parents as well as never married: teachers, librarians, accountants. For the next two years, what we did was both simple and monumental. We met at each other's homes one Saturday afternoon each month. While our kids, who ranged in age from three to sixteen, played in the basement, watched movies, or shot baskets outside, we sat in the kitchen and talked. We were all hardy survivors of the love-and-marriage wars, and we talked about our kids and our fears for them, shared what had worked with them and what had not. We went on picnics and to the beach in the summer, took the kids to the roller rink. Aaron acted as a big brother to the boys, taking them to wrestling matches and basketball games. The rest of us were occasional big sisters to Aaron's two daughters. We shared news of jobs, raises, broken hearts; we babysat for each other. Mostly what we did was consistently provide an understanding, listening ear, one hooked in instinctively to the special needs our status as single parents imposed.

The most perplexing blemish on the surface of those years was my son's inconsistent, often lackluster, performance in school. He never failed a grade, but year after year I was called to his school by teachers who complained of his disorganization and sloppiness, his playing in class and poor attention span. My son was the product of a culturally "overrich" home, yet his often average-to-mediocre performance baffled me as well as his teachers, who told me repeatedly, "He's the brightest kid in the class when he applies himself. But so often his work doesn't reflect the level he could attain."

Though Michael was clearly exuberant and highly sociable, he was not hyperactive, which would have sent me to a doctor for a diagnosis of his behavior. I was confused because at home, I watched Michael build model airplanes, read, write raps, and follow the intricate instructions of TV cooking shows with undiminished and laser-like concentration. What happened to that focus and that intensity at school? Like Michael's teachers, I simply assumed that my son was merely immature and would soon "buckle down," particularly since punishments and a strictly imposed study schedule at home seemed to have little influence on improving performance at school.

• • •

I met Joe Murray at a party given by one of the members of the single-parents group. He was a forty-three-year-old high school teacher of math and computers who arrived at the party with two longtime male friends, Issa N'dour, a Senegalese with whom he had traveled to Mexico, and Lawrence Berry, a fellow teacher. Throughout the evening, he joked and parried with these men in a way that revealed the depth of their friendship. And he approached me with no rap, no line, wearing his maleness easily, with nothing to prove. On the dance floor, he informed me that he was supposed to be in the Dominican Republic but that the host, Tina, his old friend and "play sister" who taught with him at Dunbar High School, had threatened never to speak to him again if he didn't cancel his trip and come to the party. Joe talked with me and Louise, my closest friend, who was refreshing. Though he was clearly interested, I never felt as though I was being "hit on" or assessed.

On our first date, over dinner in a Black-owned restaurant, Joe said, "I wish you'd had a chance to meet my daughter before she left for California." In those words I heard a declaration of the fierce loyalty he felt toward his family. He was the father as well of a two-year-old son whom he saw once a week. When I asked why he had never married, he told me, "I refused to get married just because other people or society thought it was time or if I thought it wouldn't last." After dinner, we drove to a street near Capitol Hill where he had just purchased a house that he planned to renovate and turn into a rental property. He told me that evening about his five trips to Brazil, a visit to Suriname, the pen pals he had all over the world. He was the kind of kid, he said, who, when he played cowboys and Indians, had volunteered to be an Indian because his parents had told him about the West from the Indians' point of view. Joe's family was close-knit, politically active in DC politics, and respected. They welcomed Michael and me into their midst as though our presence enhanced who they were.

Within a few weeks, I was beginning to love the way Joe combined a sense of adventure and a quirky skepticism in the face of conventional wisdom with a healthy respect for the practical and the secure. One Saturday afternoon, Joe spent several hours with Michael and me eating crabs, watching movies on video, and talking. He did not charge into the space I had created with my son as though it was his to remake simply because he was a man. Joe Murray won over Michael not by trying to be "Daddy" but by being himself. On Sunday, Joe often brought his son, Austin, to my house, where he played with Michael. Early in their relationship, Michael made Austin two three-foot-tall baseball players out of cardboard, painted their uniforms, and drew their features in so lifelike a manner that Austin wondered if they were real. For months, whenever he came to my house, the first thing Austin asked for was "baseball man."

•  •  •

Just as Joe and I became lovers, as I savored my son's reconciliation with his father, just as the pieces finally seemed at last to fit, my son careened into adolescence. I heard the deepening of Michael's voice, witnessed the growth spurts that propelled him to a height that echoed his father's, saw the sudden appearance of muscles—and a bikini-clad Jet centerfold plastered on his bedroom wall. I was flushed with trepidation. Soon Michael would inhabit that narrow, corrupt crawl space in the minds of whites and some Black people too, a space reserved for criminals, outcasts, misfits, and Black men. Soon he would become a permanent suspect.

Seeing him, women would think twice about entering elevators alone with him, cops would slow down in their patrol cars, watch him a little more closely when he walked down the street. Store owners would automatically assign the security guard to keep an eye on him when he entered the door. And there was nothing I could do. By the time my son was twelve, every day I wondered when he left me in the morning what would be the manner of his return to me at night.

This move by Michael into a new stage of his life made me realize more than ever how important it was to choose a boyfriend or husband who would bring his own special talents into our family circle. My son missed nothing. He witnessed my love affairs and was influenced by them. Any man who entered our life influenced my son explicitly and implicitly, providing cues and lessons and models for adulthood and manhood. After the breakup with Philip, I assessed the men I dated more carefully. It became important to know what their attitudes were toward their own family, if they had friendships with both sexes—or friendships with anyone, if they were satisfied with their work, if they were men who sought to creatively control their fate rather than sink into bitterness or complaint about what they had not achieved, if they cheered me on in my own work, if in their relationship with me they were seeking an equal partner or only a helpmate, if they felt secure enough in themselves to accept the depth of the bond Michael and I shared. One day my son would fall in love, and I wanted to teach him lessons about love that he would not have to discard or question because he found them tripping him up or ensnaring him. My love, I now knew, was also my son's legacy of love.

Joe and I discussed marriage six weeks after we met but decided to wait a year before making a final decision. Neither Joe nor Michael felt the need to compete for my affection or attention. Until Michael turned fourteen, when suddenly all adults became intolerable, his relationship with Joe was relatively tension-free. As the months passed and it became clear that Joe and I would indeed marry, I wanted Michael to tell me what he thought of the changes such a move would introduce into our lives.

"What do you think of Joe?" I asked him over dinner.

"He's an all right dude." More and more with each passing year, the youngster who despite average grades had scored two grades above his level on standardized tests resorted to vague generalities, shrugs, and grunts, even groans, to express himself.

"Okay, you've got to translate for me. Just what does that mean?" I asked, giving Michael my I-mean-business look as he reached for a glass of water.

"He's okay."

"Only okay?"

"You know what I mean," he said, shrugging for the third time.

"No, I don't. Tell me what you like about him."

"Aw, Mom, do I have to?" he moaned, as though I had asked him to endure the Chinese water torture.

"Yes, you do."

"Why?"

"Because we're getting married."

"I knew that," he said, unimpressed.

"You did?"

"Sure."

"How?"

"I could tell."

"How?"

"I just could. I'm only thirteen, but I'm not stupid."

"That means he'll be your stepfather. And you'll have a sister in Keesha and a brother in Austin."

"Uh-huh." He had dived back into the food on his plate.

"Can you handle that?"

"Sure," he said, giving me an are-you-kidding stare.

"You can?"

"Sure. Joe's a decent guy. I mean, like, he works all those jobs. He's got two houses. He's done stuff." I could hear the respect that Michael would never openly admit.

"So you think he'll be able to take care of us?"

"Sure."

"What are we going to give him?"

"What do you mean?"

"Well, we'll get this all right dude as a father and husband. And we'll get his kids and his family that already treats us like kin. What will we give him?"

"I don't know."

"You can't think of anything?"

"A perfect son and a beautiful wife."

"That's obvious." I laughed. "But what else?"

"I don't know." Another shrug.

"Our love. Our loyalty. Our respect."

"I knew that." He grinned smartly.

"You may not ever love Joe like a father, Michael, but if you give him half a chance, I know you can respect and honor him as somebody who cares about you. That's all I ask, okay?"

"Okay. Don't worry, Mom. I think you picked the right one this time."

# Trouble the Waters

The decision made during the fall of Michael's ninth-grade year to send him to a private boarding school was born of years of frustration in the face of lackluster, indifferent grades from an obviously bright and talented child. I had taken him out of the public schools once before when he was a fifth grader, and enrolled him in an excellent private academy whose curriculum was Afrocentric-based. But even there, with smaller classes and more one-on-one attention from the teachers, Michael still performed with less success than intelligence and other standardized tests indicated he could. As the prospect of high school neared, I felt a radical step had to be taken. Greater structure, a more rigorous curriculum, and a setting where there was no reward from classmates for disruptive behavior had turned around the sons of friends. I hoped that such a change would get Michael on the right track too. In addition, a boarding school began to seem an attractive alternative as the violence in the schools increased.

• • •

In early January of 1993, I decided to keep a diary. This would be the year that Michael would see his father and that he would possibly go away to school. I wanted to freeze and permanently possess the events and emotions that would define that year in my son's life. I kept a diary as well to meditate on and overcome the psychic toll imposed by the continuing murders of Black youth. Washington, DC, was becoming a killing field. A diary would provide me with a space where the blood did not flow, could not reach me, although its pages in time were consumed by my struggle to understand why death enthralled so many youngsters, why it seemed more seductive than life.

### JANUARY 6, 1993

Went to the library today and looked through a guide to Independent Schools, trying to get a sense of options for Michael. I also called two of the schools Audrey

73

Chapman's sister-in-law suggested and asked for catalogues. Susan Shreve told me about a Quaker school, Westtown, outside of Philadelphia. The headmaster there was formerly at Sidwell Friends. Susan says he took her son under his wing when he was going through a difficult time and helped him a lot.

I'm definitely going through with this, feel I have no other choice. My son is running out of time and chances. Michael's behavior in the fall term was inexcusable. We got a call from his science teacher reporting that he had loudly and for the raucous entertainment of the entire class mocked her Indian accent. The assistant principal called one afternoon to report that Michael had cursed at her, and as usual there were the requests from several teachers for conferences to discuss Michael's behavior and poor performance. Nothing seems to work—groundings, no television, no phone calls—nothing induces a change in behavior or performance. That's why a boarding school has begun to look attractive as a possibility. Michael is screaming for structure and a kind of discipline neither the public schools nor Joe and I can provide. But I still feel some discomfort in all this. I remember attending Columbia University for graduate school and the often primitive racism behind the school's elite ivy-covered walls. I know that the stereotype of the prep school as a haven for spoiled rich kids from conservative homes is outdated, but what is the reality, and is it one that will fit my son? In bed last night, I lay for a long time beside Joe, curled into a fetal ball, missing Michael already, wondering if we could find a school that had enough Black kids so that he would feel comfortable. Last night Joe and I talked about where the money would come from to send Michael to a boarding school (the money somehow always comes). And we talked as well about interracial dating, or as I put it, "the white girl issue." My professional and personal life is interracial and often cross-cultural, but I still view my son as a resource for the race; with the distressing statistics Black women face when seeking a mate now and in the future, if I can produce a healthy, successful Black man, I want him to partner with a Black woman. We talked about all this and more, and yet still concluded that any girl Michael brought home would be judged on her character and not her skin color.

## JANUARY 8, 1993

Sat down this evening and surveyed my finances, what's coming in and what's going out this year, and it appears that I can afford to take Michael to Nigeria this summer. Femi and I have talked often about a possible trip in our calls, and he has frequently mentioned this in his letters. For a variety of reasons, I feel this summer is the right time. I think this first trip, two weeks is long enough. No way can we make up for all the years lost even if Michael stayed a month. But at least this year I'll do what has been long overdue.

## JANUARY 10, 1993

The brochure, video, and application form from Westtown arrived in the mail today. The video is instructive and entertaining, but it's hard to know how much is reality and how much is PR. The financial aid form is a book in itself, is terribly intrusive, and asks for more data than the Internal Revenue Service. I doubt we'll qualify for aid, but I want to give it a shot anyway. Michael, still sulking over the prospect of attending boarding school, refused to look at the Westtown video this evening.

## JANUARY 18, 1993

This morning I called Nigeria and spoke with Femi, told him about Michael's behavior in school, which earned Michael a 6 a.m. transatlantic lecture from his father. We talked about my plans to visit him this summer with Michael.

## JANUARY 19, 1993

Went to B. Dalton today and bought several books for Michael to read, including Bloods by Wallace Terry, Black Boy by Richard Wright, The Chocolate War by Robert Cormier, Tiger Eyes by Judy Blume. He may be a slacker at school, but I refuse to let him slack off at home. I plan to give him two weeks to read each book and then give him an essay test on each one.

## JANUARY 21, 1993

Michael's campaign to dissuade me on the boarding school issue continues. Tonight it consisted of an attempt to discuss it with me "reasonably," with promises of better grades and behavior. When I told him it was too late, I was subjected to "The Look," a gaze of utter, total contempt that involves a tight muscular pursing of the lips, a trenchant rolling and simultaneous narrowing of the eyes. Part of The Look also involves a steeling of the body and a quick, dismissive turning away from the subject that presents the back full-fledged, embellished by hunched, angry shoulders. I have had it with The Look and grabbed him by the collar—yes, at five feet two, I grabbed my five-foot-eight son by the collar of his T-shirt, yanked him up close into my face, and told him that I would slap The Look off his face the next time I saw it. We stood eye-to-eye, nose-to-nose, me staring up at him, him staring down at me. He was so furious, I could feel the anger on his skin, and in the midst of this, in the middle of the most horrid look on his face, I saw a tear roll down his cheek. I let him go then, for I felt such a cataclysmic mix of feelings, I started shouting at him to go to his room. And I didn't want him to possibly see me cry.

## JANUARY 22, 1993

I talked with Jake for a while in his office at the Male Youth Program at Shiloh Baptist Church today. He explained the weight training program that he is designing for Michael. Then he told me that the staff took a poll of the boys in the program last week, asking what they feared most. The majority of the boys said, more than anything else, they feared being shot. Some of these kids routinely hear a symphony of gunfire riddling the air outside their homes at night. Former Mayor Marion Barry was in attendance at the program this afternoon with his son Christopher, who is enrolled. Barry, decked out in African-style clothing, looked good, clear-eyed and healthy. It is so hard to measure how the program is impacting Michael. But at least I know where he is after school, I know that he is supervised by caring capable adults and that his energies are being directed into positive outlets.

The Male Youth Program, begun by Shiloh in response to the increasing violence that ensnared so many young Black boys on the streets around the church, consists of an after-school study hall, supervised weight training, basketball, field trips, classes in computer literacy, and snacks and dinner. The program director, Jake Roach, is a veteran youth-development counselor who was a senior staff member of former Mayor Barry's Youth Leadership Initiative, one of the most successful programs of the Barry years. The outreach program trained the brightest young teens in the city in community service, academics, athletics, and leadership skills.

I asked Joyce Ladner once why the Black church had not done more in response to the crisis facing so many of our young people. Taking a deep breath and shaking her head, she told me, "You may not believe this, but given the mentality, the deeply rooted conservatism of many of these churches, they've done as much as they can."

"I don't accept that," I told her. "Look at how slow the church was in responding to the AIDS epidemic in our community, and as far as I'm concerned, they are still asleep on the issue of our youth, drug abuse, and crime."

"Remember," she continued, "the Black church is deeply rooted in the Protestant ethic and an essentially fundamentalist faith. The men and women who fill those churches on Sunday morning get up Monday through Friday and go to work, they pay their taxes, they obey the law. They fear God. And they simply cannot conceive of drug abuse, homosexuality, youth crime, teenaged pregnancy, and AIDS as resulting from anything other than a lapse in morals. They made it, they'll tell you, so why can't the young people. And they made it against odds that would make the younger generation tremble."

"But the church builds housing for the poor and elderly, sets up soup kitchens," I said.

"Yes, and the people affected by those services aren't carrying guns. Often the ministers and deacons are as afraid, as terrified, of the young boys on the street as we are. And so many of the young people now have virtually no connection to the church, whereas a generation ago somebody took you to church on Sunday so you were part of the community that the church created. All this makes it that much harder for these congregations to reach out to many of the people in our community most in need."

But at Shiloh, Reverend Henry Gregory had, a decade earlier, called together the men of the church after one Sunday morning service and with them had looked out his office window onto the grubby streets surrounding the church. Although the fashionable cars of the affluent congregation filled the streets that day, Reverend Gregory urged the deacons and others gathered to see instead the poverty and the violence that festered and grew inside the homes on many of the blocks adjacent to the building in which they stood. He charged them to build a way within Shiloh to save the young boys of the neighborhood. Noted sociologist Andrew Billingsley attended that meeting and told me, "When a Black Baptist minister gives you an assignment, believe me, it gets done."

Now at Shiloh, in the crowded basement space the program shares with a day-care center, Jake and his staff create an atmosphere where young boys feel safe. Jake regularly visits the schools attended by boys in the program to talk to teachers and counselors. He takes youths in potentially dangerous situations into his home while seeking social-service help for them. His staff of young male assistants is as dedicated and devoted as he is.

## JANUARY 23, 1993

When Joe and I married, Michael and I moved into Joe's house on Eighth Street in Northwest Washington. The block is one of early-rising, hardworking middle-class Black professionals who battle dirt and crime with a combination of political savvy, righteousness, and community spirit. It is a street where neighbors have known each other long enough to report misbehaving youngsters to parents, who are grateful for the information, and where seniors, many of whom have lived on the block for decades, are accorded the status of respected elders. There is the requisite young white "homesteading" couple, who have renovated a house across the street from us. They of course are harbingers of the gentrification looming on the horizon. There are one or two families on welfare, but they are integrated into the life of the street as firmly as everyone else. Cleveland Elementary, one of the best schools in the city, known for its intense parental involvement, claims the corner adjacent to our house. And around the edges of Eighth Street, there is drug traffic.

## JANUARY 25, 1993

This morning when Michael left for school, with Joe and I sitting in the car watching him walk down the street, we talked about Michael's adoption of the "gangster walk." He has begun to walk in the style that when we were young was called "pimping," a slightly cocked, rhythmic, almost three-quarter-beat mini-stagger young Black boys have long adopted for camouflage and protection. The walk says, "Don't f*** with me"; it asserts, "I'm cool"; and at its most hostile it says, "Beware." Shaking his head as he watched Michael walk toward the subway at the corner, Joe worried that he is simply overdoing the "cool pose." So intent on signaling that he is "cool" with his walk, Michael, Joe feels, is inadvertently signaling vulnerability, that rather than fitting into the neighborhood, he doesn't belong.

Joe worries that Michael will become a victim of his own unpolished bravado. I know that Michael lacks the steely inner core his gyrations imply he possesses. We both fear the consequences of a misreading of Michael's body language. If only these kids weren't armed to the teeth, if only they couldn't buy a gun as easily as a bag of potato chips, if only, if only, then we would worry less.

Since we moved onto the block, Michael has managed to navigate his way each day through the small knots of "drug boys" that claim the neighboring blocks, and he shoots ball and rides his bike with all the boys on the street. There are no hard-and-fast boundaries in the Black community. Even in the middle and upper classes, most of us are merely one generation away from poverty and one paycheck away from hard times if we lose our jobs. And so it is inevitable and even perhaps mandatory that Michael learn to say "What's happening" to the drug boys on Ninth Street and a polite "Hello" to Mr. Woods, our Neighborhood Advisory Council representative and the unofficial mayor of Eighth Street, when he passes by.

## JANUARY 26, 1993

The daily death toll recorded on the pages of the Washington Post is controlled by a mysterious, primal, almost gothic aesthetic. The accounts of young Black males shot over a look, an imagined slight, turf, or a girl become a kind of literature, a never-ending, fascinating, horrible, unfolding saga. I yearn for the stories to end, yet find myself reading them obsessively in search of a new tale, a new death. Joe comes home from Dunbar in the afternoon with accounts of a handful of unruly, potentially lethal students who can create havoc all out of proportion to their numbers. The days when he could break up a fight are over, for now students are armed and could hurt him for not allowing them to settle a score. And because it gets dark by five, most evenings I drive three blocks to pick Michael up from Shiloh; I am that afraid for him.

## JANUARY 27, 1993

Have scheduled interviews for two private boarding schools, St. Andrews in Delaware and Westtown, for next month.

## JANUARY 28, 1993

This evening we were gathered after dinner in the living room. Joe sat switching channels, and several images from Black Entertainment Television filled the screen, videos featuring, as they nearly always do, light-skinned, long-haired girls as the objects of affection, lust, and desire. The three of us span the color spectrum: Joe, light-skinned, what we used to call "redbone"; me, brown-skinned; Michael, caramel-colored. We have talked frankly, openly, about color in our house, about everything from why blondes are typecast as innocent/dumb/good to why darker-skinned Black women most often play asexual roles and darker-skinned Black men criminals and heavies. Yet tonight, when Joe grimaced in disgust at the preponderance of light-skinned girls and the virtual absence of darker-skinned beauties in the videos, Michael shouted, "You all always act like it's a conspiracy. It's no conspiracy that the girls look like that." We ended up arguing for fifteen minutes.

Later in the evening, when Joe turned to "For the People," a weekly show featuring interviews with Black historians, Michael laughed, "Everything was invented by the Black man, right? The Black man was the first one to invent the salt shaker!" Part of the program at Shiloh divides the boys into age groups, each named after Black men of note, and the boys get a heavy dose of Afrocentric education. This evening, Michael gloried in refuting everything Joe and I believe. Maybe we never really agreed. Maybe I took my son's silence as assent. Joe says he's just drunk on testosterone.

## FEBRUARY 4, 1993

This evening, Michael and I went to Woodward & Lothrop to buy a suit for the visit to St. Andrews. Michael has decided now on a go-along-to-get-along tactic, abandoning his staunch, outspoken resistance to boarding school. I wonder what strategy he will spring on us next.

## FEBRUARY 5, 1993

Michael came in from Shiloh this evening and headed straight upstairs into our bedroom, where for forty-five minutes he and Joe talked. When I asked Joe if there was a problem, he told me Michael had wanted to talk to him about something that had happened at school. Just before he went to bed, I cornered Michael in the kitchen and asked what was going on. It seems he is having a "problem" with a boy at school hassling him. He talked to Joe about what to do and how to handle the situation. When I asked why he didn't come to me, he shrugged and said, "You'd just get upset, but Joe, he knows what to tell me to do."

## FEBRUARY 8, 1993

This morning, we drove up to Middletown, Delaware, for Michael's interview at St. Andrews. He was handsome in his first real suit—a double-breasted dark green jacket with a light yellow shirt and silk tie. During the two-hour drive, he finished The Chocolate War. We talked about the moral dilemma the young hero faced and why he chose to handle it the way he did. We talked about what Michael would have done in the same situation. We also discussed the Judy Blume book, which I chose so he'd have to relate to a female protagonist. He said he liked Judy Blume's books because she "tells it like it is."

We arrived forty-five minutes early, and after finding out where the administration building was, we ate lunch in a nearby diner. Michael said he was nervous about the interview, worried that he wouldn't do well. I tried to assure him he'd be okay. My son could charm a safe open, could talk his way out of hell—would that he'd turn some of that skill to study habits and writing papers.

The nearly pastoral campus of St. Andrews was the setting for the film Dead Poets Society. The buildings have the look and feel of a monastery. Our guides, as I had requested, were two young Black students. St. Andrews is an Episcopal coed school. Boys wear ties and jackets. Mike's guide was from Brooklyn, my guide was from a town an hour away from the school. A thin, serious, young biracial student, he told me when I asked him about the racial atmosphere at the school that he felt more comfortable at St. Andrews than he had in the public schools. At St. Andrews, he told me, he wasn't teased by Black or white students as he had been in the public schools because he was biracial. And he spoke of finding a greater sophistication about the issue of race at St. Andrews than he had honestly expected.

We toured the huge gymnasium and the indoor pool; I saw the science labs. The facilities for the students were expensive, impressive. After the tour, Michael had to write a short essay and then was interviewed; then the admissions director spoke with me. I was told that for the tenth grade, there are only five positions open. I'm not sure Michael will be accepted. During the drive back home, Michael marveled, "The boy who was my guide was pretty nice. I thought the kids there would be like robots or nerds." When we arrived home, the results of the SSAT test Michael had to take for St. Andrews and Westtown had arrived. I was almost afraid to open the envelope. He scored in the upper-fifty percentile, a good solid score. This score gives him a fighting chance at admission. But what does it really mean? Mostly that he is a product of an upper-class background and is familiar with the language—the jargon of standardized tests—and has a facility for testing well. It doesn't mean he's smart, and I reject it as a predictor of his future performance academically or in life.

## FEBRUARY 13, 1993

Joe and I drove out to Mitchellville, Maryland, this afternoon to look at houses. We really want to stay in the city, but the cost of a house in a suburban-type neighborhood in Washington is simply astronomical. Mitchellville is quiet and clean, with lots of Black folks. Has been profiled in the N.Y. Times and on local news programs as an upper-middle-class haven where Blacks supposedly purposely choose to live rather than with white folks. Joe and I just want a large house we can afford in a clean, relatively crime-free neighborhood, and despite the media implications, I'm sure that's all most of the Blacks who live out there want. Little do white folks know that we really don't eat, drink, and sleep their perceptions of us, or tailor the most important things we do as a reaction to them. I've spoken with people who live in Mitchellville who say it is quite racially mixed. But for the media pundits and observers, the sight of so many well-off Blacks in one place raises the "self-segregation" or "conspiracy" bugaboo. As we drove around developments with names like Paradise Acres and Lake Arbor, Joe wondered aloud, "Now tell me what these people do wrong. Everybody always talks about the Black middle class selling out, not giving back to the community. What is their crime? That they get up and go to work every morning and stay out of trouble?" We talk often about the way in which middle-class Blacks are lambasted by other Blacks for their success and how whites cite that success as proof that racism is dead. I "give back" as part of my own political and spiritual lifestyle. But why can't just living a decent life, raising a morally sound family, be considered giving back too?

The homes are large, we saw several couples out jogging or walking together to stay in shape, and people waved as we drove past.

## FEBRUARY 14, 1993

Michael turned fifteen today.

## FEBRUARY 15, 1993

Tonight Michael and Joe had a standoff. The issue was the sloppy condition of the bathroom after Michael has been in it to shower or bathe. Michael gave Joe The Look and edged almost nose-close to Joe. Joe warned Michael to be careful and then simply pushed him away. Michael left the room. Joe refuses to lay a hand on Michael as punishment, saying simply, "I don't want to do that." I hear in his voice the hint that if he ever did, even with my approval, something might change between him and Michael so unalterably for the worse that he does not want to risk it. Joe has worked with young people all his professional life and tends to put more faith in imposing discipline and in reasoning than in physical punishment. He is my husband, but he is not Michael's father, and he knows this in a way that

I sometimes choose to forget. I've talked with stepparents who've acknowledged that bonding with a stepchild is neither easy nor inevitable.

## FEBRUARY 17, 1993

After school today, Michael and I took the train to Philadelphia. Tomorrow is Visitor's Day at Westtown, a full day of activities and programs for students applying to the school. Because the day will be so full, I wanted us to get a good night's rest rather than have to get up so early to drive up from DC. We'll take the commuter train to Westtown, thirty miles outside Philly, in the morning.

## FEBRUARY 18, 1993

Woke up to find an inch of snow on the ground. The commuter trains to the suburbs were delayed. While waiting in the train station, Michael and I read The Book of Questions, which proposes various ethical and moral dilemmas and asks how you would handle each one. It was fascinating to hear Michael grapple with questions like, "Would you add one year to your life if it meant taking one year from the life of someone in the world selected at random?" Michael said no, vehemently. When asked, "If you could choose the manner of your death, what would it be?" Michael responded that he didn't much care about the manner of his death as long as he had "a chance to fight for it." I liked that answer a lot; listening to Michael, I learned that he is more thoughtful, and more brave, than I suspected. Today I remembered how and why there was a time when Michael may have been in some ways my best friend.

Westtown has a completely different atmosphere than St. Andrews. Here there is no dress code. And when we entered, the jeans, the fades, and the casual style of students made it feel like a regular high school. I was struck immediately by the multiracial and international character of the student body. Most of the Independent Schools have on average a 5 to 7 percent Black student enrollment. Westtown has 11 percent. There was a warmth, an openness, at Westtown that I liked immediately. Michael turned indecipherable during the visit, lapsing at moments into his "cool pose," so I could not tell what he was feeling.

We took the tour of the campus. My guide was a young Black girl from New York who told me, "I like Westtown a lot, especially because I don't have to play the role of the stereotypical Black for the white kids or the Black kids." That evaluation spoke volumes about the kinds of identity conflicts our kids get wrapped up in and are sometimes destroyed by.

After the tour, Michael was interviewed. Then I was interviewed. During my interview, Susan Wiggins, the associate dean of admissions, told me, "Your son just bragged about you being a writer; he's so proud of you." I was surprised, for Michael never says anything of the kind to me. I was honest about Michael's spotty record but was assured that academic performance, while an important factor, is not the only one weighed in admitting a student. Then I met the headmaster, Tom Farquhar. We talked about how the school handles conflicts between students. Disputes are settled through negotiation. Fighting is simply not allowed. Students who fight are expelled. When I asked what Westtown is looking for in the students they accept, he said, "A student who will enhance what we have here, who will bring something to the mix." Thirty-three states and nineteen countries are represented in the student body. This is the school for Michael. I have the feeling he will get in.

## FEBRUARY 20, 1993

Michael wrote his father tonight. How will he and Femi relate to each other this summer? What will they say? Talk about? What will they feel?

• • •

African Americans exist in the imagination of America as a kind of public property, suitable for endless, invasive examination and definition. Traditionally, white scholars have built lucrative, acclaimed careers on analysis of our lives. Now it is the deaths of our sons that foist us relentlessly into an arena designed by others, where our sorrow and rage yield no protection against intrusion. We possess no private racial space in which to mourn or regroup. Dissected, discussed, but still denied full equality or justice, we see our triumphs and setbacks become the province where others ultimately reign, armed with counterfeit knowledge we fail to combat. What will this unendurable loss of so many members of a generation mean? We are the ones who must speak, who must anoint this tragedy, give it a name, a designation that holds within it the path to a resurrection of spirit, hope, and resolve.

Three weeks before Christmas, 1990, when Michael was twelve, and three months after I met Joe Murray, Jay Bias, the brother of basketball all-American Len Bias, was killed, shot outside a suburban mall in Prince Georges County, Maryland. I was at the stove, preparing dinner, when Michael yelled, "Mom, Jay Bias has been shot." We knew the Bias family from the TV screen, had seen the majestic, eloquent mother, Lonise, transcend grief, seek meaning in the senseless, cocaine-induced death of her son Len, picked the day of his demise to play professionally for the Boston Celtics. We knew the father, James, sturdy, composed, less outspoken but obviously a bulwark of the family. We knew them. We knew them, my son and I, too well.

So, when I ran into the living room, still clutching a spoon dripping spaghetti sauce, and heard that Jay had been shot, I felt that because the media had connected me so intimately to the earlier tragedy and grief of the Bias family, I had lost one of my own. Jay died a few hours later, in the same emergency room at Leland Memorial Hospital where Len had died. The same doctors who watched Len's life elude their gifted hands and training saw Jay die too. Jay Bias was killed by twenty-seven-year-old Jerry Tyler, who fired into the Jeep that Jay was riding in with two friends. Two bullets hit Jay in the back.

This was the season of grieving Black mothers, their faces a somber mural possessing and filling the television screen, their stories a fixture in the morning papers. That is how I came to know them: Cynthia Harris, whose son was headed for college in Colorado before he was killed by a bullet intended for his buddy; Patricia Godley, whose fourteen-year-old son was killed in a Northeast alley; and Lonise Bias. Michael's vibrant, always-growing-right-before-my-eyes life symbolized the meaning and depth of these women's grief. In the face of their anguish and mine, I was a writer who did not know what to say.

I still did not know what to say when Michael asked over dinner a week after Jay Bias was killed, "Why are most of the people we see arrested on TV Black?" The food in my mouth suddenly lost its taste. I had taught him to relentlessly question everything he heard or saw, including everything his teachers said, and even to question me. In that moment I reaped my reward.

"Why?" he insisted, eating still, his eyes pressing me against the wall. My answer was a lecture about history, about "the system," and about sociology. I told Michael that some of the biggest criminals were shielded from discovery or punishment. And as I told him this, the unsatisfactory sound of the words clogging my ears, I wondered, what did slave mothers say to children who asked, "Why are all the slaves Black?" I had raised my son to believe that he could do or become anything he wanted. And I sat telling him that we were nevertheless prisoners of history. I could accommodate the contradiction. Michael merely gazed at me in confusion.

"Black on Black Crime," "The Black Male as Endangered Species"—the conferences, the studies, the books proliferated, mushroomed into a self-fulfilling prophecy, an industry that fed on itself. From 1987 to 1990, nearly 1,500 people, most of them Black males of all ages, were killed in Washington. And during this period homicide became the leading cause of death nationally among Black males aged fifteen to twenty-four.

What surprised me was that I didn't grow numb. I still felt horror and outrage at the violence and death—the teenage girl who fatally stabbed a young boy because he "joaned" on her mother, the infamous videotaped robbery and shooting where the perpetrators mugged for the camera and urinated on one victim. No, the victims didn't become faceless, nameless. I was wrenched every time.

A friend of mine, a counselor who kept track of such things, told me once that twenty-one was the most vulnerable age for young men. "Twenty-one," she said, "it's like if they can get past twenty-one, they'll make it." That's when more homicides, suicides, and accidental deaths occur among young men, she said. She told me this a decade ago. Len Bias was twenty-two. Jay Bias was twenty.

When Jay Bias was killed, in my role as Michael's mother, the what-ifs seemed never-ending. The questions began in the summer before he entered junior high school. There was the mad scramble to find a school that was not just academically sound but unplagued by gangs, violence, and fights. I thought in Backus Junior High we had found such a school. But I didn't breathe easy long. One of Michael's friends was jumped by a gang of boys at a Metro subway station near the school. He did a poor job of defending himself and was lectured by his parents about self-defense, manhood, courage. It was the same lecture I might have given in the past, but now I was afraid that the trigger of a gun pulled in a split second, the hairsbreadth slash of a knife, made such words irrelevant. And I sat dreading, waiting for Michael's first fight, a rite of passage once innocent, now fraught with the possibility of death.

In November, a boy from school started calling Michael in the evening, making verbal threats. I knew nothing of this until weeks after the calls began. Then, one afternoon, I was gripped by an instinctive urge to drive by Michael's school at three o'clock and pick him up. All day I'd had a sense of foreboding, had been unsettled, on edge. I rounded the corner near Michael's school in time to see him heading away from the bus stop where he would normally board the bus for home. I saw his pumped-up swagger, his shoulders braced for battle, as he headed who knows where. He spotted me and halted dead in his tracks, embarrassed, angry that I had stolen his thunder. A quick interrogation revealed that he was headed to a nearby school and neighborhood to deal with the caller, who had labeled him a "chump." I ordered him into the car and we drove home, Michael fuming, me uttering a quick silent prayer that I'd caught him in time.

Pride and courage matter, and so my admonitions about nonviolence and negotiation rang hollow even in my ears. Joe and I talked to Michael that evening about contacting parents, about never going into unfamiliar neighborhoods alone to settle a score. As we watched Michael go upstairs to bed, Joe concluded, "He's got to defend himself, he can't let these kids walk all over him."

Joe had told me that whenever there was a murder on the streets or in the clubs of DC, the teenagers he taught at Dunbar inevitably knew the victim and the perpetrator. Having seen so many young men whom he had taught murdered in the past several years, Joe said he could now tell which ones wouldn't make it. "The ones who won't listen to anybody, who think they know everything, who've got a quick temper, they're doomed." And what of the innocent victims of these boys? Neither of us really wanted to talk about them.

So the next day, he told Michael, "When you're in public, watch how you walk. Don't bump into people. Don't stare. You're tall, but you've got an innocent face, and that sends a mixed message to people looking for trouble. People can tell you're a good kid just by looking at you, and they'll mess with you just because of that." The unscathed openness of Michael's demeanor was proof that he had been a protected, loved child. But this same quality was also suddenly a liability, one that he had to mask. As I listened to Joe lecturing Michael on how to present himself in public in the presence of other Black males he did not know, I was reminded of the admonition of Black parents in the South to their children to "never look a white person straight in the eyes." I thought, too, of the countless mannerisms and poses, of the complex ruses of language and speech that African Americans had fashioned over the years to maintain a sense of dignity while standing before the withering, unseeing glance of a white person who deemed them inferior. Now my son had to develop a vocabulary of body language that would serve and protect him in the midst of his own.

When I picked up the extension one evening and heard Michael say "shit" and "damn" in conversation with a friend, Joe told me, "He'd better know how to use those words sometimes. There are situations on the street and at school where knowing how to use those words could save his life."

In the spring, Michael joined Little League. The coach and his wife were dedicated to the adolescent boys they worked with three days a week and molded into a solid team. In the middle of the season, however, they played a game at a Southwest housing project, one of the city's toughest. During the game, the opposing team threatened to use bats on Michael's team if they were beaten. A neighborhood resident brandished a gun on the edge of the field. The spectators, rooting for the project team, became so threatening that the police were called to escort Michael's team off the field when the game ended in a tie.

In the months following the near riot on the baseball field, an insistent disbelief came over Michael that I was glad to see. I wanted him to be frightened when he should be, I wanted him to know that, even against the blood-drenched tapestry being woven from top to bottom in this society, violence and guns were not supposed to be the norm. I would have shuddered had the violence evoked in him absolutely no response.

• • •

I had wanted to meet Lonise Bias since the death of her oldest son, Len, had transformed her from a seriously religious suburban mother and bank executive into a charismatic, fervent evangelist on a crusade to save young people on the verge of trouble. And so, because I have always used language to try to explain the indecipherable, to heal and to transcend, I proposed a story on the violence racking the Black community to a local magazine, and for this story interviewed the Biases. When the television appearances began in the aftermath of Len's death, Lonise Bias's dignity, her anger, and her passion made me think that if Sojourner Truth or Harriet Tubman had lived in an era of mass media, they would have sounded like her. I wanted to meet her to discover how a mother says of her son's death, for a ten-second sound bite, "God took the best to save the rest." How many sleepless nights, how many tears, how many tranquilizers, how many prayers, bring you to the point where you can say that? God took the best to save the rest? I wanted to meet Lonise Bias because I wanted to know: How do you survive hell?

I knew that Lonise Bias thought that after Len died she and her family were safe. Fate, God, or whatever would never be so cruel as to take another one. I knew what the Biases had experienced, but I still wanted to know what pulled them through. For I had thought about Len as I watched Michael prepare for bed, and then I was thinking about Jay.

At the time of his death, Len Bias was a commodity, a valued asset of the Boston Celtics, the most historically successful and prestigious team in the NBA. Len Bias was a star. Red Auerbach, president of the Celtics, had said that no rookie player in Celtics history had ever inspired the anticipation that Len Bias sparked. Len had signed a lucrative contract to endorse Reebok athletic shoes. He was, at the age of twenty-two, a legend, and like all legends, he appealed to a kaleidoscope of wishes and needs in the collective psyche of a public that claimed and devoured him. He was the son of a devout, upstanding middle-class family; he was the "down" brother who, despite his dizzying talent on the court, remained accessible, popular, well-liked; a stylish dresser, he wore expensive suits as though born in them. A Black Horatio Alger, Len Bias was a success in a way that everybody could understand, and he was or would soon be a millionaire. On the basketball court, he was astonishing to watch as he turned the game into an art form. He was going to be the next great one.

Already in the Promised Land, Len Bias was merely waiting for the rest of us to catch up.

On one level, the story of Len's final night was very simple. A group of young men gathered in a room in a dormitory at the University of Maryland to celebrate Len's contract to play with the Boston Celtics, signed earlier in the day. The young men celebrated with beer, cognac, and an ounce of 88-percent-pure cocaine.

Len's death is symptomatic of a culture that glamorizes chemically altered states while paying lip service to fighting chemical dependency. That night, Len Bias's last night alive, is a commentary as well on youthful bravado and the invincibility the young feel is theirs by right. Len and his friends could just as easily have been white students at Brown or Berkeley. What was Len Bias a victim of? His own bad judgment or arrogance? For ultimately, Len Bias chose to celebrate his victory with drugs and alcohol. Not all of his fellow teammates indulged. He could have, as his father hoped, spent that night at home with his family after they arrived from Boston on the shuttle. But he did not. One of Len Bias's closest friends, Brian Tribble, was with him the night he died. It was Tribble who frantically dialed 911 when Len collapsed, unconscious. The following year, Tribble would be acquitted of charges that he had provided the cocaine that allegedly caused Len Bias's death. Yet in the fall of 1993, Tribble, long known on the streets as a mid-level drug dealer, would be sentenced to ten years in prison for his role in a major cocaine distribution ring that operated in Washington, Maryland, and Virginia.

And what of Jay? Certainly, he was much more than Len's younger brother. Jay was, in his mother's words, "the one who's suffered the most because of Len's death." Jay graduated from Northwestern High School, where, like Len, he was a star on the school's basketball team. Although he was highly recruited, Jay failed to get the necessary 700 points on the SATs, which made him ineligible for a Division One scholarship. So he attended a junior college with a strong basketball program. He left after a year to work and to consider a four-year college and was thinking of entering American University. But his application to AU was turned down because he lacked sufficient transferable credits. Friends say Jay was losing interest in basketball. He had worked, upon returning home, in the dining facility at the Collington Episcopal Life Center in Mitchellville,

Maryland. And he worked, at the time of his death, in the mailroom of a local bank.

How was it to be Jay Bias, Len's brother, when Len was alive? When he was dead? The wife of Jay's killer alleged during her husband's trial that Jay had been pursuing her romantically for months and that his attentions bordered on harassment. Jerry Tyler said that was why he shot Jay, to keep him away from his wife. Jay's friends said that Jay's last words before he died were the Lord's Prayer and a plea for them to tell his parents he loved them.

Did Jay ever dream of his own death? I am sure he dreamed about Len. What were his secrets? What were his fears? At twenty, Jay Bias must have wanted more than anything to find a way to be a singular, brazenly bright light, unconnected to the trail left by his older brother. At twenty, I am sure he only wanted to be Jay. But what we remember is that he died too soon, just like Len.

When Lonise Bias became a national figure, an overnight spokesperson on the plight of the nation's troubled youth, inevitably there was a postponement of the grief that she and her family felt. The process of grieving over the death of a loved one consists of days that go on forever, unfamiliar sorrows, the desire to be touched, held, listened to, the need simply to be left alone. In reaching out to the white, Black, brown, and yellow children of America, magnificently shaping her pain into an altruistic impulse that could only be admired, did Lonise Bias unknowingly deny Jay the chance to privately mourn, aided by her considerable compassion and skill? The turn outward, the move into the public sphere after Len's death, made sense of the senseless. Might a move inward, a closing of ranks and the family circle, have strengthened Jay, enabling him to grieve and grow and to more clearly find his own way?

It was imperative for me to meet James and Lonise Bias. We owned their son Len, whose triumph and death became public spectacle and process. So, too, in the same manner did we own their grief. But I wanted mostly to meet the Biases so that with them, I, too, could mourn—mourn with them the loss of two sons whose deaths had made me hold my own son closer. Our community, scrambling for answers and safety, unsure and under siege, lost resources, intelligence, and hope in the instant of Len and Jay Bias's deaths—as in the instant of all such deaths. I sat with the Biases as the Jews sit shivah, as grieving African mothers pray and offer food to carved wooden dolls representing their deceased children, I sat with them to speak the names of their two sons, to never forget.

The Bias home was located on a quiet, well-kept street in Landover, Maryland. James Bias greeted me at the door. He is a dark-hued man, friendly, easygoing, and solid. We sat for a few minutes, breaking the ice in the tastefully decorated living room. We discussed the weather—it was May and yet the temperature blazed like August. I didn't know what I expected, but not this peace, the tranquility that filled the spotless house.

Lonise Bias came upstairs from the basement. She is a tall woman who wears her height gracefully. They had just returned from a vacation in the Bahamas. An easy camaraderie, an emotional synthesis, joined this man and woman, honed during more than twenty years together. The death of a child is supposed to destroy a marriage. James and Lonise Bias sat before me, the strength of their union palpable, living, breathing in the room with us. The interview began with a prayer initiated by Mrs. Bias. I rose from the sofa in response to her outstretched hand, her tall frame filling the living room's space. We stood with our hands clasped while the sonorous voice of Lonise Bias sought divine intervention in what would pass between us. By the time I sat down, I knew how they had pulled through. They were born-again Christians possessed of a bedrock faith relevant to every aspect of their lives.

Since Len's death in 1986, Lonise Bias had lectured at colleges and high schools in forty-seven of the fifty states. She showed me a stack of letters from students and administrators praising her talks, giving her credit for turning young lives around. There was skepticism from some at first, she said. "What do you know?" they asked. "Your son was an addict." She does not accept this conclusion.

But the death of Len gave her a vision, she said, forced her on a mission to reach young people and their parents before it was too late, before drugs and violence filled a void parents feared to approach. And who was better qualified than she to speak? she reasoned. Her talks mixed a back-to-basics approach with a willingness to listen to and hear her young audiences. When she first started the lectures, she found that after she talked about Len's death, the young people lined up by the hundreds wanting to talk to her about a host of problems unshared with parents or other significant adults in their lives. So the letters, the hundreds of one-on-one conversations, had taught her what she called the six lies young people in America live by, the same lies that derail them.

Her voice whirring up like an engine, Lonise Bias ticked off the lies on each finger: "If I get all the material things, I'll be okay. If I join the right group, I'll be okay. If I do what the group is doing, if I disrespect adult authority, if I have sex, I'll be okay. No one has a problem like mine."

I sat rapt, as enthralled by Lonise Bias's presence and conviction as the hundreds of young people she had addressed. I realized that she was conducting a ministry, that she had been called to speak and to guide, and, that like all healers, she had tapped a spiritual genius that awaited her obedience and her touch.

The young friends of both Len and Jay still filled the house, stopped by to visit, bringing their girlfriends, their children. "This house is never empty," she told me. "It's always filled with young people who loved Len and Jay."

Of the past and the present, she said, "For twenty-two years we were just an average family, raising our kids to be the best they could be. We were close-knit. Nothing we experienced came close to this. I didn't realize what a problem drugs were until Len died. God strategically prepared me with a certain strength to go through all this. This isn't strength that's rational or that comes from man," she said.

Still, there was disbelief. James Bias said of Len, "You never imagine your son could die on a college campus."

In the days following Jay's murder, James Bias appeared publicly on Capitol Hill testifying in support of the Brady Bill and held a news conference with Jesse Jackson in support of gun control. I heard it more in the voice of James Bias—what had been lost here, the price the family had paid. I wanted to inquire, but found myself unable to ask how the two other Bias children, Michelle and Eric, had handled this double loss.

Gerald W. Eiland, the driver of the car from which Jay was shot, had been sentenced the day before our meeting, and I asked them their feelings. "I felt no vindication," James Bias said, shrugging. Lonise Bias said, "It's all a waste when a young man is sentenced to thirty years." What neither of them said was that even a life sentence wouldn't bring Jay back. And that they were still sentenced to a life without him.

(In the spring of 1993, a Maryland Appeals Court overturned the conviction and the life sentence of Jerry Tyler and the thirty-year sentence of the man who drove the car from which Tyler had shot Jay Bias. The court ruled that the prosecutor had violated the state's equal rights law when he used peremptory challenges to bar women from serving on the jury solely because of their sex, reasoning that they would feel more sympathy for Tyler. Yet it was a jury of eight women and four men that convicted Tyler. In a retrial that took place by the end of the year, Eiland's conviction on second-degree murder and related handgun charges would be overturned by a jury that after three hours of deliberation found him not guilty. Jerry Tyler was found guilty of murder in his retrial in the spring of 1994 and sentenced to a prison term of life plus twenty years.)

I closed my notepad and turned off the tape recorder, and the conversation drifted to where we as a nation and as a people were headed, how things had gotten this bad, who bore the blame? James and Lonise Bias and I talked of pride, crime, family, and the days before integration when segregation enforced a cohesiveness and a unity purchased with other political rights. We didn't long for those days, but wondered at the unevenness, the bitterness, and the dissatisfaction of the exchange. Before I left, we stood once more in prayer.

• • •

The Biases were children of God, good citizens. What more, I knew they might ask, was there to be?

• • •

## FEBRUARY 23, 1993

This afternoon Michael went to the movies with two friends. Before he left, I gave him the lecture I have learned from Joe, told him how to handle himself in public. He is growing so fast that he is suffering growing pains in his arms and legs and does not know how to handle or control the body sprouting faster than he can adapt to it. I told him if he and his friends went into any stores, to stay in plain sight of the salespeople and to leave any bags they enter with at the counter.

## FEBRUARY 26, 1993

Tonight I was called by a parent of a Westtown student who lives in Reston, Virginia. The school asked her to call me to discuss the school parent-to-parent and to answer any remaining questions I might have. She was affable and pleasant, and we shared adolescent war stories. Her son is a year older than Michael, likes Westtown, and has done well there. Near the end of our conversation, she mused, "But you know, sometimes I'm a little afraid, he's up there in the woods of Pennsylvania, anything could happen." Little did she know how eager I am for Michael to attend a school in a setting like that. For on the streets of our neighborhood and in the halls of Michael's school the "anything" this mother merely fears and cannot name is a reality we know too well.

## MARCH 3, 1993

We looked at a house in Mitchellville today. It needs a bit of work but is large. Once we give it a paint job and put down hardwood floors, it will be perfect. Joe is leaning toward putting a contract on it.

## MARCH 4, 1993

Joe and I went to dinner tonight with Steve and Carol, and I described my frustration with Michael's behavior in school and his grades. Carol said that Michael sounded a lot like their son, who has a learning difference called attention deficit disorder (ADD) which results in an inability to be attentive for long periods, forgetfulness, and poor performance of rote assigned tasks. She suggested I get a diagnosis from a doctor at the National Institutes of Health, a Dr. Alan Zametkin, who treated her son and is a leading specialist in research on ADD.

## MARCH 5, 1993

Michael's "girlfriend" called this evening. As far as I know, it is a telephone and school romance. If there have been dates, I don't know anything about them. In the age of AIDS and STDs, I'm glad that the phone is their most potent form of communication. I have never met her. Know only her name—Sophia. I wonder what my son finds attractive in a girl? Has he had his heart broken yet? Will he be a generous thoughtful lover/husband/friend to women?

## MARCH 9, 1993

Joe and I went to a movie this evening, took the subway. On the way back, at the Metro Center stop, we met a former student of Joe's. Joe has taught preschool, junior high, high school, and adult education in DC for the last twenty years. And we regularly meet former students when we are out, for he has helped to educate a generation of youngsters in the city. The young man we met was a student of Joe's when he taught at Lincoln Junior High School. The young man was well built, friendly, open, and there was a deference, a respect he accorded Joe and me that I don't often see in young people. He has graduated from high school and is studying to be a member of the DC police force. When Joe asked him about Lonnie, Melvin, Antoine, and several other boys who were in the class he taught with this young man [as a student], to each name the boy said, "He's dead" or "He got shot."

Eight of the twenty boys that Joe had taught in that class have been killed in gang or street or criminal violence. Even Joe, streetwise and difficult to surprise, was stunned. We stood in the subway station disbelieving, shaken. "Well, how'd you make it, man?" Joe asked as the young man's train approached.

"I saw the others getting killed, and I decided I wanted to live, no matter what. I made choices different than theirs," he said.

As we watched him board the train, smiling and waving goodbye, I wondered if it really was that simple. I know for some it is, but for others who live in neighborhoods so violent they'd be fools not to carry a gun, the choices are a conundrum. And standing beside Joe, who was still shaking his head in amazement, I remembered the former female student of his we'd met a few weeks earlier who told Joe about the students in her class. "Mr. Murray, the girls got babies and the boys are dead."

## MARCH 11, 1993

Michael received a letter from Femi today; enclosed was a photo of his four-year-old son, Yemi. The boy has a strong, almost fierce personality that I could almost feel as I looked at the picture.

## MARCH 25, 1993

We heard from St. Andrews. Michael's application was rejected. He didn't seem too upset. I think he wants to go to Westtown, though he will not admit it.

## APRIL 5, 1993

An admissions officer from Westtown called today and informed us that Michael has been accepted. He has fought and resisted this outcome, and yet when I told him and we talked, he could not conceal his pride.

## APRIL 7, 1993

It's been a month since Carol suggested I contact Dr. Zametkin. He sent me a packet of diagnostic forms for Michael's teachers to fill out describing his behavior in school, answering questions about attentiveness, completion of work, disruptiveness. But the teachers I gave the forms to two weeks ago filled them out as though they were recommendations for college; they praised him to the skies and downplayed all the problems they have complained about to me. I nearly wept when I collected the forms from the teachers. I had fully explained what the forms were, why we needed them. But they are simply of no use, no value, and yet they remain the primary evidence used in diagnosing the disorder. Michael's teachers are so burdened with huge classes, paperwork, bureaucracy, it was all I could do back in February to get them to write the recommendations for Westtown for him. But I feel especially frustrated because if ADD has been hampering Michael's ability to achieve, I want to get on with the diagnosis and treatment strategy. But I will wait until he enters Westtown and get the teachers there to assist in the diagnostic process.

## APRIL 9, 1993

Joe and I took Michael to dinner and a movie tonight to celebrate his acceptance at Westtown. It was a good evening, we were all relaxed, easy with one another. Joe beamed in pride and could not resist a friendly lecture not to "blow" this opportunity. While we waited for our order, we congratulated Michael with a toast. As he placed his glass back on the table, however, he said, "Now I just have to make it through the summer without getting shot."

## APRIL 28, 1993

Today was my birthday. Joe and I closed on the house in Mitchellville, and one of Michael's friends died of a gunshot wound, allegedly while playing Russian roulette.

Adedayo Ayodele and his family lived next door to us when we lived in an apartment complex in Northeast near Catholic University, in the days when Philip was a part of our life. His parents were Nigerian, and I remember "Adayo" (his nickname), which everyone called him, as a terribly smart, very aggressive, but troubled young boy who had been kept back twice in school and was frequently suspended because of fights. I remember, too, that the neighborhood kids teased him because he was very dark and because he was African. This is the second boy whom Michael knows from the old neighborhood where we lived for five years who has died a violent death. A year ago, a young boy named Rico who had attended Backus with Michael was killed three blocks from his house on his way home from a New Year's Eve party.

When we talked about Adayo's death today, Michael said when he approached the school steps this morning, he saw some friends outside and they said, "Hey, man, guess what?" He told me, "I thought, 'Oh no, not Adayo, don't tell me.' And then they did, they told me Adayo was dead. I cried."

All evening Michael was upset, confused. "It makes me feel like if God could just take somebody like that, He could take me," he said.

There was an assembly at Michael's school this morning to deal with the students' feelings about the death of Adayo. Michael is angry that no one can explain to him why this happened. How do I tell Michael that God did not take Adayo's life, that Adayo, if he indeed was playing Russian roulette, put his own life in danger. But the story sounds very strange to me. I told Michael that whoever owned the gun bears responsibility too. But at this moment I think it is easier for Michael to believe that "God did it."

As Michael was packing newspapers for recycling tonight, as he washed dishes, we talked about Adayo.

"God created us with free will, Michael."

"Yeah, tell me anything." He shrugged bitterly. "God let this happen!" he shouted. "That's what you mean by free will. God let Adayo be killed."

"I don't know, Michael," I said, reaching to hold him, to verify and confirm his life in my arms. "Maybe that is what I mean, maybe it's all I can say."

## APRIL 30, 1993

Michael told me that at school today two of the boys involved in the incident with Adayo told him the Russian roulette story was a lie. Apparently Adayo and several other boys, all on suspension from school, were in the home of one boy playing video games. Another boy came into the house and brought out a gun to show them. When he put it close to Adayo's face, the gun fired. No one knows if it was an accident or murder. The boys told the police they'd been playing Russian roulette as a cover story. I feel in some ways as empty inside as Michael. I lived next door to Adayo and his family for five years. And I have tried to compose some words to say to his mother. What can I say when I feel so ashamed, so angry? I feel ashamed remembering how the boys in the neighborhood, according to Michael, teased Adayo relentlessly about his name, calling him a "dirty African," calling him "Black" and "monkey." (These same boys and children at school had teased Michael so much about his Nigerian name, Akintunde, that he begged me to let him use Michael as his first name.) I feel angry that the culture of violence in America made this boy less safe in what his parents literally viewed as the land of opportunity than he would have been on an unpaved road or in any home in any part of Nigeria, an allegedly "less developed" country. I called Backus and got the address of the family and sent them a card. The thought of hearing this grieving mother's voice was too much. I am not as brave as I thought I was.

## MAY 12, 1993

I am in Yellow Springs, at Antioch. Tonight I called home, and Michael and I talked about his prom for graduating ninth graders, which is tomorrow night. Joe will take him and Sophia to the dance and pick them up. I wish I could be there.

•••

A sometime mentor and friend, Joseph Jordan, director of Antioch's newly established African-American studies program, arranged my monthlong residency at the school when my classes at George Mason ended for the semester. Like many African-American professors on white campuses, Jordan served double, sometimes triple, duty as professor and as surrogate parent, counselor, and friend to the Black students at Antioch. The office of the African-American studies program had become an unofficial home base for Black and other students of color.

Again and again during my visit, when I asked, professors and administrators at Antioch told me there was no "typical" Antioch student. "They come from all over, and their backgrounds range from the old monied to the persistently poor," one colleague said. But with their studied casualness, and with the desire of most of them to work in fields that would allow them to change or at the very least impact society and the world, Antioch students were a special breed.

In my writing workshop, the students wrote about pivotal men in their lives. I was amazed that when given a chance to write about themselves, the class chose instead to consider and rediscover fathers whom they had never met, or who had died too soon, or from whom they were estranged; or a son who, in a moment that may never be understood or overcome, took his own life.

The only male in the class was a young man named Marc, who was the most sophisticated and ambitious writer. At twenty, he was wiry, thin, ebony-hued, and wore a nose ring. He brought to the first class copies of a long prose poem about his mother, a work that he would in the weeks that followed transform into a fierce and simply brilliant essay on his father, and on himself.

The poem, one of many he had written, was too long and awkward in parts, but I knew immediately he could write. When I told Marc this after the first class, he looked at me in genuine surprise, shifting uneasily as he stood before me, the eyes behind his Ben Franklin lenses uneasy, disbelieving. I recognized the look. I had seen it before on the faces of so many young Black students, so bright and so sharp that they were almost dangerous, and yet they simply did not believe this. So I told Marc to come to see me during my office hours. The words he wrote on paper had pulled me into the seams of his life. I wanted to know more.

The relationship I developed with Marc during my weeks at Antioch, becoming friend as well as teacher, reflected my style of teaching and evidenced my own hunger to hear a sensitive, articulate young Black male voice. For back home in Washington, Michael woke up many mornings a stranger to me. The house crackled with tension as he struggled with me and Joe to wrest identity, autonomy—life, it seemed, sometimes—from our sphere of influence. I talked to Marc hoping he heralded the future voice of my own son.

The youngest of three sons, Marc grew up in a Philadelphia neighborhood called West Oak Lane in Germantown. He was unashamedly devoted to the mother he credited with keeping him out of trouble, and maybe even alive, by encouraging him to read and stay off the streets. The father he admitted had bequeathed him his humor, playfulness, and dark skin was a source of anger, anguish, and discomfort, their conflicted relationship fueling much of Marc's best writing. In his spare time that semester, he was reading Jack Henry Abbott's rage-filled scream from behind prison walls, *In the Belly of the Beast*, and George Jackson's prison diary, *Blood in My Eye*. He admired both men, he said, because of their intellectual transformation behind bars. One of his cousins, Andrew, had been jailed in Pennsylvania, and the writer in Marc was eager to know what his cousin endured and how he could survive and possibly come out a better man. When he visited me in my office, we talked about crime, about punishment and redemption, the standard definitions of each and the definitions that life, unpredictable, often unjustly imposes.

During one of our many conversations, Marc told me that his SAT scores and high school grades were unimpressive; as he told me this, I thought of the fraudulent measures of this society for gauging intelligence and worth. I remembered, too, the bitter joke Joe had told me that asked: How does a Black college athlete raise his SAT scores? Answer: By checking white on the box marked RACE. Joseph Jordan and Elaine Comegys had told me that Marc's adjustment to Antioch had been rocky and his evaluations (given at Antioch in lieu of grades) inconsistent. But like me, both felt that when this young man became a "finished product," he would be awesome.

Marc and a close friend, Ren, also from Philly, arrived at Antioch born-again Christians. His mother was a devout Baptist, and shortly before coming to Antioch, Marc renewed his faith, even vowing to be celibate until he married. But after a year and a half on campus, he had found his views of faith, morality, and religion evolving and changing, sometimes radically. Time alone spent reading and thinking, conversations with other students, and especially traveling around the country meeting and working with people from different backgrounds—travel facilitated by the Antioch system, which combines academic semesters on campus with off-campus work experiences called "co-ops," which take students all over the country—all conspired to challenge and revise the orthodoxy of his faith.

Marc and I discussed the final draft of his essay during a session in my office one afternoon. I suggested several minor changes and edited the manuscript with him watching over my shoulder. His essay rivaled the work of some of the graduate students I taught at George Mason University full-time. Then we talked, as we frequently did, about books and reading, the process, the joy and discovery of it all. The weather in Yellow Springs had been fickle, and that day it was chilly, overcast. My small office was damp as a cave. My wall-length window revealed the campus, green but sodden from three days of rain. The class had already met for the last time. I would leave the next day. In this conversation with Marc, I asked him to tell me about his past, his present, and even tried to nudge him into the future.

"Did you miss hanging out on the streets with the other kids as a child?" I asked. "I was pretty scared to hang out with them. I just had this intuition. I knew, for example, if I hung out with my brother's crowd, I was going to get into something I didn't want to get into."

"What was happening on the streets?"

"Break dancing, turntables, and rapping. People would do that and get together on the corner. There'd be house parties, street parties. But I wasn't interested, so I went out with my small group of friends. And we'd always have to be headed somewhere. We couldn't just hang out on the corners, because just hanging out, there was always the possibility of trouble."

Marc spoke of "trouble" as easily, as banally, as Michael described the invasion of his school by armed thugs. Marc's voice was flat, unemotional, as though "trouble" were something that, at twenty, he knew and no longer feared.

Marc told me that his brother Corrie had been "in more trouble than he's willing to tell me about," and had been part of a group whose worst members had killed men and were now in prison. Corrie had been lucky, Marc said, for he was never involved in any criminal activities, although he was prepared to take the blame for a friend who beat up someone on the subway. "He was going to take the rap for this guy. I don't know how he got out of it, but he did. My mother was pretty upset with him."

"Why do you think he was willing to do that?"

"Well. Corrie's friend assaulted a guy with a pair of nunchakus that belonged to Corrie. When the police came, the others had left and Corrie was the only one on the scene, with the nunchakus in his hand. He didn't want to be a snitch. The charges were later dropped."

"Any other reasons?"

"I know some of those guys, and my brother and them had been in fights together and they had each other's back. And when you're in a situation like that, I guess you kind of fall in love with your friends, you feel they must be your real friends. But that's an illusion."

"Do you ever feel endangered?" I asked, wondering how young Black males responded to such labels.

"When I was growing up, I always felt a fear of hanging out in the street. I know," he said quietly, "that I felt fear. And I wasn't really thinking about the future."

At Antioch, Marc's horizons had expanded considerably, stretching far beyond what he viewed as the claustrophobic hold of his Philadelphia neighborhood on his sense of possibilities. Marc's co-op assignments had included working at the Amos House soup kitchen and homeless shelter in Providence, Rhode Island, at a shelter for teens in San Diego, and at a group home for autistic children in San Francisco.

"Tell me about the co-ops, what were they like?"

"When I went to some of my jobs, I had dreadlocks down to my shoulders, not cut short like my hair is now. Usually I got the job, but some jobs, they didn't hire me with dreadlocks because of the myth that the hair is dirty. Things like that the school really doesn't tell you about. They expect you to learn that on your own. The jobs I think I will have in the future will probably be live-in residencies with disabled citizens. That's something I'd like to do. I may have some trouble with clients' families. They may be a little bit racist. I had a problem with one lady because I was a man; I don't know if it was because I was a man that she didn't want me taking care of her daughter in a home for autistic children. I might have a problem with that. Some families might not want a Black man to take care of their loved one."

When I asked about his fears for the future, Marc said that he worried less about himself than about his three younger cousins who lived in a tough area of West Philadelphia. Their stepbrother was jailed in Florida. And even then, Marc was unable to reconcile the crime for which his cousin had been imprisoned, shooting and paralyzing a man, with the soft-spoken cousin that he had always known. Several months later, when Marc and I spoke, he told me that his cousin, like his brother, had taken the rap for a crime someone else had committed. The maze of allegiances and loyalties that bound these young men to others so firmly that they would sacrifice personal freedom gave me pause, made me wonder who was really paying for what and what "crimes" each supposed "innocent" had committed, perhaps on his own. I knew that protecting family and friends was also a strong motivation in cases like the one Marc described.

I wondered also what Michael would do if ensnared in a moral labyrinth such as this one, and prayed he would never have to make such a choice.

"You told me that you write your cousin Andrew in jail. When you write to him, what do you say?"

"I send him poetry, he sends me poetry. We were real close growing up, and I guess I'm trying to get back to that time and place with him. I ask him a lot of questions about what it's like in jail. But he doesn't tell me much."

"What do you want to know?"

"Well, I guess I sort of want to be a witness in a way. I feel like no matter what I do, something could have happened and I'd have ended up where he is. But I didn't. I want him to know I'm with him. I don't know, maybe I'm not in jail because he is."

"And your cousins?"

"I worry about them because they're attracted to the street life. So I'm turning them on to drawing, giving them my old comic books to read and draw from like I did as a kid. The oldest cousin is getting turned on to African-American history. He's thirteen and just read *The Autobiography of Malcolm X*, and it really affected him. I'm proud of him. He even wrote a letter to President Clinton asking that Malcolm X's birthday be made a national holiday."

"You say you are afraid for your cousins, but you weren't afraid for yourself?"

"Well, yes, I wanted to get out of Philadelphia. I felt like if I was going to die, I didn't want to die there. I really wanted to leave. I was afraid I'd get caught up in the street life if I didn't. Several of my cousins are in prison. It's like in my family, with so many of the men, they either end up in the army or in prison, and I decided I didn't want to go either place. My oldest brother, Brian, he's trying to become a corporate lawyer, and he's getting married this weekend. I don't know, he seems like he's trying to forget the neighborhood. But he says he's putting a lot back into the community. His church does that a lot too, so I trust him."

A subtext of much of what Marc had shared with me in our conversations was his desire to be of use to his community. When I asked him about this, he said simply that he didn't want to forget the community, especially the poor. And yet it was important for him to leave Philadelphia, he said, because "I felt like I was in more spiritual danger than physical. I needed a broader view of my life. Philadelphia seemed to be all there was to my life."

We talked about his father, briefly, hesitantly, and while I watched Marc shift nervously in his chair as I probed him on this subject, I recalled the stunning, visceral scene in his essay describing a beating he received from his father after he broke one of the man's bowling trophies, how his mother came to his defense and his father began to brutally beat her as well. I remembered, too, how near the end of the piece, his father stuttered in rage at Marc as he arrived home from work one day, "You don't know what it's like out there, but one day you will." We even discussed his skin color, his voice tinged with regret as he acknowledged the years of self-hate that he had felt for having inherited his father's Black skin rather than his mother's lighter hue.

"I never really liked being dark," he said. "My brother and I used to stand in front of the mirror and compete to see who was darker. And all of us men, my father and my brothers, used skin lighteners."

Suddenly he was animated, as though this admission had charged and strangely freed him, and the words were coming fast, unselfconscious, in a steady stream. With an abashed laugh, he said, "It got so bad at the end I even put it on my ass. I put it on my knees. I put it on my toes. Put it all over my body. That's how bad I wanted to be light. My father had that hang-up too. I mean, like, I never went in the sun in the summertime. I stayed in the shade. I was scared of getting even darker. My fear of getting darker helped me stay in the house during the summer. The city gets violent then, so my fear of getting darker kept me in the house and out of trouble too. So I was, like, a hermit. You know, I just recently realized that I have never dated a dark-skinned woman, mainly because since I never liked my skin, why would I date someone who looks like me?"

I looked at Marc, still dark despite years of skin lighteners, and saw a strikingly handsome young man. The watchfulness of his eyes, the smoldering intensity of his demeanor, the grace with which he carried his lean body, all imbued him with a charisma of which he was, I thought, totally unaware. Yet his anecdotes sparked memories of my mother's family, which was rabidly color-conscious. Like Marc, I, too, had had to grow up and away from the influence of home and family, flirt with and find other values in order to begin to love my Black self.

"When did you finally realize you are a good-looking Black man?" I asked, grateful for the chance to stroke his ego, hoping that he knew I meant it, hoping, too, that he really believed it.

"Books I read, like Malcolm X and Black women writers, and I just started coming to terms with it. And talking to people here on campus, and my friends. Talking to other dark-skinned people and even light-skinned Blacks. It was funny, how one person wanted to be darker 'cause he felt he wasn't Black enough. I really couldn't talk to my family about this."

"Do you think of yourself as an American or an African lost in America?"

"I don't think of myself as an American, because I lack broad experience."

"What do you mean?"

"Like, I haven't been anywhere. But if I'm outside of America, like I'll be this summer, I guess I can see it for what it is. I mean, I can read about it, but in many ways it's like reading about a distant country, it's still an abstraction, and I'm inside that abstraction. But if I get outside of it, I can see it clearly. Right now, I haven't gotten the full feel of how or what it is to be an American."

"Well, that's an entirely justified answer, I think. Our experience has been so painful here, so ambivalent."

"And lots of times I feel angry 'cause I'm confused. The more I read and the more people I talk to about their experiences, the more angry I feel, and I just don't know what to do with this anger, so I just, you know, get rid of this energy through some sort of artistic channel."

Soon it was time for Marc to head to his next class, but before he left, I made him promise that he would continue to write. I hugged him and walked him halfway. I headed back to my office alone and thought of his two brothers who had escaped the fate of their friends, and who, like Marc, were forging themselves into adults who could carry their own weight.

I admired Marc's compassion for others, his willingness to look deep inside himself even when, and especially if, it hurt. I hoped my son would one day have those qualities. I hoped he had them now. All the way back to my office, in my head I heard the mental tape of a conversation with a close male friend, Clyde McElvene, a man with whom I had worked on various projects, a Black man who was consciously struggling every day to challenge the traditional definitions of maleness and of race. One evening we talked about sons, and he said, "You tell a girl to be careful, you tell a boy to stay out of trouble. The irony is that this implies that the boy controls his fate and the girl is given hers. We live in a society that, day in and day out, perpetrates crimes against Black males, and we as a community never tell them that they are supposed to be protected."

## JUNE 5, 1993

Joe is as excited about our plans to go to Nigeria as are Michael and I. He has talked with Femi's brother Bade several times on the phone and likes him a lot, has sensed the generosity and kindness in the man. This trip has been in the making since the day I sat down to write Femi. If I had not been prepared to stand on Nigerian soil again, I never would have written the letter. There have been times in the past three years since our reconciliation that I've thought it best to wait for Femi to come to the US to visit us. But the idea of me taking Michael to his father, to the place where he was born, yes, back to Africa, quickly rooted in my heart and displaced any other possibility. I have always known a journey back to Nigeria with Michael is the only meaningful way to close the circle of questions and longing my son will always carry until he sees his father. Michael seems unconcerned, relaxed, as the day of departure arrives. He said he told Moe and David that he was going to Africa and the idea seemed amazing to them. When he told them that his father was Nigerian, that he was born there, he said they acted as though he had said he was from Mars.

## JUNE 8, 1993

Tonight I drove Michael's friend Demetrius home after they returned from seeing a movie at Union Station. When we got back home, we sat up and watched Arsenio Hall and Alfred Hitchcock reruns on cable. He told me about a paper he had to write for a project at the Male Youth Program. The paper was on Shaka Zulu, the South

African warrior king. We sat eating popcorn and talked about leaders like Shaka, Stalin, and other men who could move, shape, and forge nations and history.

## JUNE 14, 1993

Bade called this evening, elated over the results of the presidential election in Nigeria. Moshood Abiola, a wealthy businessman and philanthropist, won. He is a Yoruba and a Muslim, and Bade says he has learned from the family in Nigeria that Abiola won support from all regions of the country, a real triumph in a nation where tribal loyalties are as deeply entrenched as racial loyalty is here. The military ruler, Ibrahim Babangida, who has "run" the country since taking over in a 1985 coup, is scheduled to step down. I wish I felt as certain as Bade that this election heralded real change. I simply won't believe the military will return to the barracks until it happens.

## JUNE 25, 1993

Talked with Bade tonight about Babangida's annulment of the presidential election results, alleging widespread voter fraud and misconduct on the part of the two parties, parties whose platforms he wrote and whose candidates he handpicked. Bade says he will be demonstrating in front of the United Nations next week with other Nigerians to protest the military's action.

## JUNE 26, 1993

Michael and I got immunization shots for the trip to Nigeria today. And on the way back home, we stopped and got something to eat. I brought up the subject of our impending trip to Nigeria and asked him if he was anxious or nervous in any way. He said he wasn't. Then he said, "I wonder what I'd be like if you and my father had stayed together, how I'd be different if I'd grown up in Nigeria."

"Well, we'll find out in a few weeks."

"Was he a good man, my father?"

"Yes, he was, but there were things I needed that he couldn't give me."

"What things?"

"Well, you know how Joe and I talk a lot about things, talk about what we feel, how we spend time together, well, your father wasn't able to do that with me. He was closed a lot of the time. And I think his concept of what marriage was supposed to be was different because he was Nigerian."

"Well, then, what did you like about him if he was that way?"

"He was hardworking, ambitious, smart, and handsome, and there were times when he appreciated me and made me feel good, but we were just too different."

"You and Joe are different."

"But not on the most important things, not on the things that we feel we need from each other."

"Did my father have other wives?"

"No." I laughed. "I wouldn't have married him if he had."

We finished our meal and got back in the car and headed toward home. I confessed to Michael that I'd had difficulty sleeping the last few nights. I am not worried, but anxious, excited about the trip to Nigeria. I have not seen Femi in over a decade. A girlfriend told me she thought I was one brave sister to take Michael to Nigeria like this. She doesn't know how much I have prayed and meditated, hoping to bless our journey from start to finish, hoping to keep us safe, and hoping, too, to find for my son that the love I feared he had lost was intact, was still strong.

## JULY 8, 1993

There were massive demonstrations and rioting in Lagos to protest the annulment of the presidential election results, with scores of people killed and hundreds arrested. I don't want to cancel our trip, but I will see how the situation looks when we are ready to leave. There is a sense in which political instability, nascent or active, is a fact of life in a country like Nigeria, but I am not willing to risk our safety, and Joe will not let me.

# An Acquaintance with Grief

Crime and punishment loom, twin, inescapable shadows on the landscape of African-American life. The most tenacious folklore of racism and European-defined history defines the Black man as a crime against nature. For centuries, it was criminal for an African American to learn to read, to escape slavery to freedom, or to compete in business with whites. The legacy of this censorious past includes punishment, the Scottsboro Boys, lynchings, a system of justice that metes out different punishments for Black and white, and prisons that warehouse Black men. So when a Black youth "gets in trouble," inevitably the pull of generations of dead weight, as well as an awesome déjà vu, color a mother's expectations and fears.

When I heard the knock on the front door that evening, I wondered if Michael had forgotten or lost his key. It was seven-thirty. Basketball practice at Shiloh, I assumed, had gone on later than usual. When I opened the door, I saw Michael clutching a plastic bag from Peoples Drugstore. A policeman stood on either side of him.

"Ma'am, is this your son?" one policeman asked, removing his cap almost apologetically as he spoke.

"Yes," I told him, standing in the doorway, utterly disbelieving what I instinctively suspected.

"Well, he was caught shoplifting in the Peoples Drugstore on the corner there. The manager called us to the scene."

"Shoplifting?"

"Yes, ma'am."

Michael stood, hunched and grim-faced, between the two policemen, avoiding my eyes. Before I could ask what he had taken, the policeman continued, "The manager told us that they'd suspected him of stealing before, and tonight they caught him. They let him go this time. Said they wouldn't press charges. But if he enters that store again, he'll be arrested."

"All right, all right, I understand," I told them. But did I?

"Goodnight," I said, watching them close the gate to our yard behind them as Michael brushed past me and slumped on the sofa.

I didn't know what to ask first—what he had stolen, or why. Michael clutched the bag from the store and sat stonily before me.

"Tell me what happened."

"I went in the store," he began in a tiny, cowering voice I had never heard from him before. "I had to buy some school supplies." He held up the bag as evidence. "And I had gotten everything I needed, pencils, pens, paper, and then I saw some baseball cards on a counter near the notebooks. I wanted them. I put them in my pocket. Then I went to the cash register at the front and paid for everything except the cards. When I was walking to the door to leave, one of the security guards stopped me. I denied it at first, then when they called the police, I admitted it."

"How much did the school supplies cost?"

"Five dollars and something."

"Did you have money for the cards?"

"Yeah."

"Why'd you steal them?"

"I don't know," he said.

"Had you tried to steal from the store before?"

"Only once. Small things, nothing big."

"Why?"

"I don't know."

I sat before my son, envisioning him behind bars at Lorton, Riker's Island, or Attica. Was this a youthful, fleeting burst of rebellion or the beginning of a career in crime? I knew that the "typical" shoplifter in America was a fortyish white suburban matron, not a teenage Black male. But at that moment, that hardly mattered.

I wondered where he had stolen from before and not been caught. Michael seemed as dazed, even confounded, by what had happened as I. There was no defiance; no bravado or even hostility. I sensed shame and something he would never acknowledge—relief.

My son knew right from wrong. And he knew that people paid for crimes they committed, especially Black youth.

"The size of what you took doesn't matter, Michael. Theft is theft, and at this moment you sit before me as a thief. You know you're lucky, don't you?"

"Yeah, I know that," he said in a hoarse whisper, shaking his head, still refusing to look at me.

Even as Michael sat before me, I saw the edge of a dollar bill peeking from his pants pocket. Had he felt in control, powerful, grown-up, at the thought of getting something for nothing?

"Michael, I don't ever want you to do something like this again. If there is a next time, the manager won't drop any charges, I'll see to that. And you know what that means.

"Go on upstairs and wash up for dinner," I told him.

That night, Joe and I decided to ground Michael for two months. Michael had come closer than he realized, and closer than I wanted to consider, to suddenly having a juvenile record. That thought frightened me as much as the fear that one day I might visit Michael in some jail, somewhere in America.

• • •

The case of Terrance Devonne Brown, a Roosevelt High School honor roll student and track star convicted of first-degree murder, infiltrated my life with a subtle, pervasive insistence. For a variety of reasons, I became interested in pursuing some deeper understanding of the seeming contradiction the case presented—the young man judged by some to be exemplary and by others nearly demonic—and of the mother who had raised him alone. The same day that Michael was notified of his acceptance by Westtown, Terrance Brown was sentenced to life in prison.

The shoplifting incident was three months old. And I reflected on the day of Terrance's sentencing that his mother, Ella Ross, and I had shared the hope that education would ensure our sons lived prosperous, productive lives. Ella Ross's hopes were now shattered. Mine remained intact. So it was love for my own son that drove me to decipher the puzzle and tragedy of the son of a woman I did not know.

Terrance had quietly stalked the periphery of my life, both as a former student of my husband's and as a mentor in Shiloh's Male Youth Program under the tutelage of Jake Roach, where Michael came to know him. During Terrance's trial for murder, Michael came home from Shiloh Baptist Church each evening in a virtual daze of confusion. Michael, like most of the youngsters in the program, could not fuse his memories of Terrance—well-mannered, thoughtful, friendly, and clearly favored by Jake, who cited Terrance's academic accomplishments as a standard the young boys should aim for—with the alleged killer Terrance was accused of being in a Maryland courtroom.

In time, Michael's anguish began to reflect the at first latent, then quite vivid curiosity I felt about the case. I wanted to know who Terrance Brown was on the night of April 16, 1992, the night when as he later admitted he had killed a man. I wanted to know who he had been before that night. One thing was clear and indisputable: Terrance Brown had shot and killed an off-duty policeman. The murder occurred in the midst of what appeared to be, and what a friend and alleged accomplice testified was, an attempted robbery. The murder took place the day before Terrance was to leave Washington to sign papers for a Board of Governors scholarship from Indiana University, a four-year college located in Pennsylvania. The oppositional, conflicting nature of the primary elements of the case initially seemed stunning, a young man with everything to lose committing an act that placed his future and his freedom in great jeopardy.

Christopher Ryan Johnson, a twenty-five-year-old Prince Georges County policeman, married and the father of a young child, was waiting for a friend outside the friend's home in Capitol Heights, Maryland. He stood in front of his car checking the headlights, and moments after a young man he did not know approached him, he was shot five times in the throat, back, and thigh. He died two weeks later. The young man was Terrance Brown.

I wrote about Len and Jay Bias in order to mourn. I interviewed Terrance Brown and his mother, Ella Ross, to try to comprehend the inexplicable. Mourning, I found, was in the end easier.

From the beginning, the case for the prosecution was simple: A felony robbery attempt had ended in murder. But the defense asserted that the case was as much about perception and misread signals as it was about the death of an innocent man. First of all, the defense asked, why would a young man with everything to lose like Terrance Brown choose to destroy a future more promising than anyone in his family had ever been poised to claim? Terrance Brown's defense was that he had approached Officer Johnson to offer assistance after he and a friend drove past and spotted Johnson's flashing hazard lights. Brown approached Johnson with a gun at his waist, a gun the defense said he carried for protection because of a violent feud with a classmate. Spotting the weapon and mistakenly assuming he was being robbed, Johnson began handing over his credit cards and money to Brown and then reached for his service revolver and fired at Brown, whom he wounded in the stomach even as he himself was shot several times. Brown, the defense argued, shot Johnson in self-defense.

The only witness to the events of that night was Harry Melvin Mayo, a classmate and friend of Terrance Brown's in whose car Brown had been a passenger. It was Mayo who drove a bleeding Brown to DC General Hospital for treatment and who called Ella Ross to inform her that her son had been shot. Court documents filed at the time of the arrest of both young men said that Mayo and Brown had spent the evening taking turns committing robberies. Under cross-examination, Mayo said that he had used his own gun, hidden beneath the seat of his car, earlier in the day.

Both young men were charged with first-degree felony murder. Mayo was picked out of a lineup by a man robbed twenty minutes before Officer Johnson was shot. And on the stand, Harry Mayo, who had declined an offer of immunity from the state prosecutor but who would later receive a more lenient sentence than Terrance, admitted being an accomplice to first-degree murder. He testified that Terrance Brown had approached Johnson with the intent of robbing him. In testimony that Michael Statham, the attorney for Terrance Brown, later said effectively sealed the case against his client, Mayo said, "Because somebody's father and son and husband was killed, I want to clear my conscience. I feel guilty about what happened."

Those with whom I spoke who had attended the trial said that Mayo, a more soft-spoken, seemingly less assured young man than Terrance Brown, was both compelling and convincing on the stand. Witnesses to the trial told me that Mayo's display of vulnerability, remorse, and compassion for the Johnson family (real or feigned) was more "winning" in its way than the steely intelligence and quick-witted articulateness of Terrance Brown, who presented himself, in the estimation of some observers, as "too smart" and "too confident." Two dozen character witnesses cited Brown's accomplishments, which went beyond the honor roll and the world of athletics. He had delivered food to the elderly as part of a youth program and in a twist of irony, had been proclaimed "best defense attorney" in a mock trial competition organized by the Georgetown University Law Center.

Ultimately, Terrance Brown was found guilty and sentenced to life in prison, plus ten years on gun charges. He would be eligible for parole in seventeen years but would then have to begin serving the ten-year sentence on the weapons charges. Harry Mayo pleaded guilty to first-degree felony murder, attempted robbery with a dangerous weapon, and carrying a concealed weapon. Mayo was sentenced to life in prison, but the judge in the case suspended all but fifteen years. The judge also said he would reconsider the sentence in ten years if Mayo demonstrated that he was a model prisoner.

The case of Terrance Brown cast a pall over the Male Youth Program, for Jake Roach had mentored and coached Terrance for several years, working with him first in the Mayor's Youth Leadership Initiative and then assigning him to mentor younger boys in the program at Shiloh. The two were so close that they often talked by phone several times a week about school, Terrance's weight training, and career plans. Jake Roach said, "When I met Terrance Brown, I saw a general, a physicist, a professor, and the second coming of a football star like Lawrence Taylor all in one person."

And it was Jake, along with Peter Parham, DC's then Director of Human Services and the father of Terrance's girlfriend, who accompanied Terrance when he turned himself in to the Prince Georges County police after being released on bond by the DC police who had originally arrested him. That was a day that Roach described as "one of the most difficult days of my life."

At the sentencing, the judge sternly lectured Brown, calling him a young man who possessed two different personalities, one concerned and caring, one cold and manipulative, one personality for his family and one for his peers. If the judge's conclusions held even the smallest amount of truth, then Terrance Brown had effectively betrayed a virtual community of supporters, mentors, friends, and family. I did not know whether I believed Terrance Brown was indeed guilty of felony murder, as opposed to murder in self-defense. But I knew that the insurgent, cruelly baffling nature of the events that had resulted in Terrance's imprisonment struck a chord of fear within me for my son. Every mother wonders about the secret life, the hidden yearnings and fantasies, of her children, and whether they will control them or become victims of them. And so, long before I thought of talking to Terrance Brown, I talked to his mother.

• • •

Ella Ross is a tiny woman of impressive self-possession, and it was clear soon after I met her that her emotional investment in her son was the singular and most important force in her life. Terrance was not merely a son but a chance for her to erase the horrors of her own childhood. Through Terrance's achievements she had hoped to attain a kind of grace, as well as a redemption that even her own considerable achievements may have failed to invest within her.

As I spoke with Ella Ross over a period of several weeks, it became apparent that she had taken onto herself a large measure of responsibility for the incalculable, unknowable forces that had derailed Terrance from the neat trajectory toward success that had seemed to be propelling him until the night of April 16. Her guilt was enormous, and she was dogged by deep-seated feelings that she had "failed" Terrance. Even imprisoned, Terrance dominated his mother's thoughts and actions as totally as he had when he was free.

Ella Ross worked as an accounting technician with the Department of Health and Human Resources, where she handled all accounts for the secretary of the department. She had successfully defeated the pull of a multitude of degenerative forces in her life. Through hard work, persistence, and an impressive inner resilience, she had managed to create a succession of opportunities for Terrance. One of the most twisted, tragic ironies of the story of this mother and son is that while the mother rewrote and restructured the symbols that at birth seemed destined to define her, the son was ensnared by the full intent of their horrible grasp.

Ella told me that her childhood was marked by poverty, disruption, and dysfunction. Her parents fought violently and often, and when Ella was nine, her mother left her father and lived for a short time with her ten children in a public shelter before moving into an apartment of her own. But there were frequent moves around Northwest Washington in the aftermath of evictions for nonpayment of rent.

Her oldest sister, Ruby, became a surrogate mother for the family. Ruby was independent and strong and became a model for Ella. When she was thirteen, Ella met Harry Lee Dixon. She and her family were living in the Sursum Corda housing projects, located in a Northwest neighborhood. Ella met Dixon on a summer night through some friends. He was four years older than she, drove a car, was working, and, though married, was separated from his wife. To Ella, yearning for stability and security, he seemed mature and stable. Two years later, Ella dropped out of school and moved to New York with Dixon, where he had family. They moved into an apartment and began living together. Of that period, she remembered, "I felt like I had my own identity in New York with Harry. I was happy for maybe the first time in my life. He was working steady in construction, we had a nice apartment with nice furniture, and he took care of me."

Terrance was born in Washington when Ella was sixteen, and Dixon forged a relationship with his son that was enduring and strong, one that flourished despite the cycle of drug abuse, arrest, incarceration, release, and rearrest for drug selling that became the pattern of his life after he was injured in a work-related accident. The drug abuse led Ella to leave Dixon in New York when Terrance was five and return to Washington. "I had a sister who lost an eye to drugs, I have a brother who spent fifteen years in jail because of drugs, and my father at the age of seventy-two was jailed for drug pushing, so I just have always hated the idea of drugs," Ella said.

When she returned to Washington, Ella relied on her sister Ruby for help with Terrance. By this time, the combination of motherhood and her desire to have a better life than she had known as a child fueled an intense ambition. She worked at a fast-food restaurant and at night, while Ruby cared for Terrance, attended Armstrong Adult Education Center to earn a general equivalency diploma.

From the beginning, she recalls, Terrance was special in the family circle. "And I think I tried to make up for what I lacked. When he was a kid, I could go without a purse or without clothes, but Terry walked around in forty-, fifty-dollar suits. He had the designer shoes, and that's probably where I made my mistake. I just made sure that I did for him what was not done for me."

As Ella narrated the years as a single mother, the specter of her son, now behind bars, seemed to shape each word, infect the timbre of her voice. Terrance was alive, but he had killed another mother's son. He was alive, but when she saw him once a week, he was handcuffed. The one the family thought would redeem them all had somehow betrayed them instead. And so in every line of the narrative Ella Ross wove, she sought to find the reason why. Each possible answer pointed in her mind to an excessive, corrupt, damaging quality to the love she had offered her son. Yet she, who had been indifferently loved and protected, decided to perfectly love her own child. Denied adequate food, shelter, and clothes as a child, Ella Ross grew up and did what good mothers do a million times a day around the globe: She braved a chill and darned holes in her socks so her son could be warm. She had seen good mothers on television, in the movies, read of them in books, seen them in other families, and watched her sister Ruby, only a few years older than she, shoulder responsibilities her mother could not. She had never been effectively mothered, but Ella Ross knew what society said a good mother was.

"I went to all the PTA meetings," she said, "all the track trips. I was there, participating, taking pictures. I raised money. I did everything, like I said, that my mother did not do for us." In the midst of this conversation, she spoke of having spent four hundred dollars on clothes, shoes, and cassette tapes to send Terrance in jail. I saw that for Ella Ross, caring for Terrance had become an obsession and a need that fulfilled a sense of herself as capable, powerful, in control. I wondered when she would let go. I wondered if she could.

Her life as a single parent revolved around Terrance, including getting him to school on time each day while holding down a full-time job. When Terrance was in elementary school in Northeast, Ella was working in downtown Southwest. Without a car, and living on Alabama Avenue Southeast in one of the most isolated areas of the city, she boarded a series of buses in the morning and in the evening. Weekends, too, were devoted to Terrance, taking him to Cub Scouts or Boy Scouts or to play with friends from school. During one conversation, Ella said that because Terrance was a boy, "in a way, I was kind of making it up as I went along. I didn't know how to raise a son. All my brothers were either in trouble or in jail. There was Ruby to help me, but she had girls." It may have been then that she began in a sense to live through Terrance, to make him the most important person in their world, and to willingly sacrifice, perhaps more than was required, in the name of a mother's love. The dedication seemed to pay off. Terrance was a bright student in school, one who regularly made the honor role, excelled in sports, and won scores of awards and trophies.

There was a five-year relationship with a man who cared a great deal for Terrance, but for Ella the affair was stormy and unsatisfying. And while Ella was struggling valiantly to keep Terrance away from negative influences, she was torn by the demands of his natural desire to know his father's family. And so Terrance often spent summers in New York with his paternal grandmother. Ella was frustrated, for at the end of the summer when Terrance returned to Washington, she heard in his speech and saw in his mannerisms the influence of weeks spent with tough, older, hardened street kids.

In 1984, Ella met Albert Ross. He was a bartender and was steady and capable, and he made her feel secure. But Terrance resented Ross, felt that he undermined Ella's loyalty to him, and Terrance resented his attempts to impose a stricter, more consistent form of discipline than Ella had. But four years after they met, Ella and Albert Ross were married. After their marriage, there were frequent arguments about how to discipline Terrance, and Ella admits that she was, as Albert noted, often lax and inconsistent in meting out deserved punishments to Terrance.

"When I told Terrance to wash the dishes, he'd wash them any old way. It didn't bother me too much because I figured I was going to wash them anyway," she told me. "I'd just rewash them. I didn't go into it with

Terrance. My main thing was schoolwork. Don't let a teacher call me and tell me he wasn't doing his homework or that he was absent. Then he was in real trouble."

Because Ella saw education as the way for Terrance to erase the past they had inherited from her parents and from his father, a past of failure and dysfunction, she made education a kind of mantra, imbuing it with extraordinary powers to transform. Yet Albert Ross urged that discipline and standards be imposed on Terrance in all of his activities and responsibilities, and he saw a connection between poorly washed dishes and the rest of Terrance's behavior. Stepfather and son argued frequently, once or twice came to blows, and settled into occasional periods of peace. But for Ella, "It was like there was not enough of me to go around. My husband tried to pull me in one direction, Terrance tried to pull me in another direction. I thought having a baby would ease things, but it didn't." Ella named her newborn son Albert, Jr.

The tension between Albert Ross and Terrance mirrored other conflicts in Terrance's life and behavior. "Terrance figured, you know, he'd think if there's a problem, get out there with your fists and fight," Ella explained when I asked her about several fights Terrance was involved in. He had been transferred from Dunbar High School because of a fight, and while working with Jake Roach in the Mayor's Youth Leadership Initiative, escorting a group of children on a field trip one day to the Anacostia Museum, Terrance got into a fight with a young man and threw him through a glass exhibit case. Jake Roach fired Terrance but eventually accepted him back into the program. A few weeks before the shooting of Christopher Johnson, after gambling for money in a series of card games with a classmate at Roosevelt who refused to pay the five hundred dollars he owed, Terrance beat him up as a warning to pay the debt. And so the well-mannered youth, the bona fide scholar, the star athlete, held within him a tremendous wellspring of anger.

By the time Terrance was awarded the scholarship to Indiana University, his life was one of vivid, interminable splits. Ella had found it impossible to keep him away from his father whenever Dixon was released from jail. Yet for Terrance, Harry Dixon was simply and only his father, no matter what, and his loyalty and love for the man were fiercely resistant to his mother's warnings. Terrance was surrounded by a host of male forces. In Terrance's last year of high school, Albert Ross, who loved him, had formally adopted him. Ross struggled to be a positive force in his life, even as Terrance built barriers between them. Jake Roach was a source of advice and support, but there was also Terrance's increasingly close friendship with Harry Mayo. Terrance had also begun to spend more and more time at his grandmother's house, where Ella feared anything could happen and where so many of the influences she tried to protect Terrance from were often in the picture.

But in the spring of Terrance's senior year in high school, Ella Ross may already have allowed herself to imagine attending his graduation in June and to revel in fantasies of another graduation four years hence. For her son had traveled places she had never been; he could count on community leaders and members of city government for advice and references. Academic and athletic awards lined the walls of her apartment. The scholarship he had received covered virtually all his academic expenses. I am sure that during that spring, Ella Ross more than once flash-forwarded in time in her imagination, looked back, and concluded that the sacrifices, the conflicts, and the pain had all been worth it.

• • •

## JULY 9, 1993

This afternoon, Joe, Michael, Joe's son Austin, and I drove over to Annapolis to have lunch with Aunt Bert. At seventy-five, she is a marvel, in good health, informed, sophisticated, and travels so much we can hardly keep up with her. If it is Paris, the Bahamas, or San Francisco, Aunt Bert has been there, and often with a young niece or friend or relative forty years her junior. We went to a family-style restaurant. Around the table this afternoon sat four generations.

Aunt Bert has "adopted" Austin as grandson, as she did Michael, sending him birthday and Christmas cards with money and stocking up on toys in her apartment for our visits. Over lunch, the conversation drifted to developments and changes that marked the differences between her generation and mine and between mine and Michael's. As in all conversations of this kind, we adults were pretty rough on today's kids. We talked passionately about the lack of self-respect and discipline that we see in so many young people. We talked about money, responsibility, the future.

I felt a little sorry for Michael, for he was outnumbered. But the conversation, which had Aunt Bert recalling tough times in the thirties and forties and how hard she had worked, and Joe complaining about the failure of so many of his students to really apply themselves, symbolized the fear that so many of my contemporaries share, that our children will squander what we worked so hard to gain. Sitting at the table today was my husband, who worked three jobs in order to buy rental properties. For me, work and achievement have been the way I have let the world know I am here. My dedication to language and spending long hours working with words helped pay for the house in Mitchellville and will pay for Michael's tuition at Westtown. But Michael lacks fire, the hunger that drove many of us even when we were his age.

Where, we wonder, is the hunger in our kids that drove us? This quandary is not unique to African Americans, it is the story of any successful class or group—how to ensure that their progeny build on rather than waste what they have earned. But because each higher rung on the ladder is grasped despite so many obstacles, so much we have to overcome, refute, ignore, deny, the question of what our children will do with the dream rests at the heart of the matter.

Michael's response was simply, "I can't help it that I was dealt a lucky hand."

"It's not luck," I told him, "that results in you sitting here with us healthy, strong, smart, and endowed with advantages so numerous you take them for granted."

"You all talk about rap music being bad, and the clothes we wear, but it's you, you adults, who created MTV and who sell the music and make the clothes," Michael insisted vehemently, certain he had proved our collective hypocrisy.

"All right, we do make the jeans," Joe said, "but we didn't tell you to wear them down to your knees." He laughed, breaking the tension simmering among us.

"Listen, dear," Aunt Bert told Michael, patting him gently on the arm, "your parents and I just want you to carry on and do as good as we did or better."

•••

At Roosevelt High School, they called Terrance Brown "Prime Time" because of his personality, his academic success, and his ambition. "Prime Time," as though he was already a star. But as I drove out to the Maryland Correctional Institute in Jessup to finally see Terrance Brown after having spent many hours talking with his mother, his lawyer, and Jake Roach, a multitude of thoughts unraveled in my mind and competed for my attention. I thought of the three different accounts of what had actually happened on the night of April 16. There were the rumors that had floated on the streets that Terrance and Harry Mayo had been, in the street vernacular, "doing the do"—robbing people at random—and that on the night of April 16, they finally got caught. I thought of Mayo's confession. Some argued that the confession was merely the untrustworthy narrative of a young man facing separate robbery charges who betrayed a friend to gain a lighter sentence. In any event, the jury clearly believed Mayo's version of the events of that night. Are guilt and remorse automatically erased from the emotional vocabulary of a young man because he may have committed a crime?

I thought as well of Terrance's assertion that he was a good Samaritan who had been mistaken for a thief, and I considered how people who knew him said such an act of assistance would have been consistent with the Terrance Brown they knew. However, I couldn't shake a friend's nagging question: "How could a young man who had never fired a gun before outshoot a trained police officer and hit him five times unless he'd already had his gun drawn first?"

And Ella Ross had acknowledged that "yes, a life has been taken, yes, some time has to be served," in the letter she wrote to the judge pleading for leniency, a letter that led the judge to sentence Terrance to ten years instead of twenty for the related gun charges in the case. I wondered if the confidence that Ella Ross had so lovingly instilled in her son had turned instead into a sense of invincibility that made him feel he could rob at will and head off to college the next day.

Terrance's lawyer, Mike Statham, talked with me about the trial and about Terrance; making Ella Ross a symbol of so many Black mothers, he concluded, "Our women have had to face so much. We are the only race on earth that asks our women to lead the race out of bondage, and they simply can't do that alone. I see so many Terrances, and when these Black boys are in trouble, they come into my office with their mothers.

The mothers always come, the fathers are never there. And it's then that these women ask me to talk to their sons, talk to them the way some father, some man, should have long before they were sitting across from me. And often by then, it's too late."

Statham's words were heartfelt and clearly impassioned, but too neat, too unmindful of the complex, unruly task that parenting becomes in all families. Jake Roach talked to Terrance several times a week and saw him almost every day. Albert Ross had cautioned, had tried to intervene. These were no absent, indifferent, shiftless, or lazy Black men. Instead, caring, concerned adults wished for Terrance's success, even more than he did, if that is possible. And Ella Ross had led her son away from the bondage she had known, the bondage of poverty, the fear that you are not safe, secure, and loved. Ella Ross did everything right, yet somehow her son still lost in the end.

As I drove out to Jessup that day, I still did not know if Terrance Brown was a murderer or the victim of a more than cruel twist of fate. I did not feel any longer that awareness of his guilt or innocence was mine to search for or claim. But I still wanted to see if I could gain some small measure of knowledge about who he had been and who he was now. And I promised myself that would be enough.

We talked in a small room off a noisy corridor near the entrance to the prison. The first thing that struck me was how young he looked. Ella Ross had given me pictures of Terrance at different ages, and in all the pictures, I saw immediately his steely confidence; however, sitting across from me was a nineteen-year-old youth who was really still a boy. Very dark-skinned, tall, he wore a stylish shirt, with jeans that were fashionable and expensive. His smile was expansive, almost heartbreaking in its radiance. Terrance still had unflagging friends and supporters who visited him. Peter Parham, the father of his former girlfriend and an official in city government, still came to visit him regularly, he said, and girls from Roosevelt came to visit him too.

When I asked him how he was holding up in prison, he told me that to get through each day, he had tried "a little bit of everything. I've even tried yoga. Sometimes I laugh to keep from crying." When I asked if he had changed in any way since his incarceration, he said, "I feel more bitter, I don't trust people as much as before. I feel like it was a betrayal of trust that got me here. I mean, like, I feel betrayed by Harry, and even though I'm sorry that I killed that policeman, I went up to him with no bad intentions. He just assumed I did."

When he first arrived in the prison, because he was considered a cop killer, the other prisoners showed him a deference, a respect, that chilled and shamed him. "They let me use the pay phone before others, or threw me the basketball as soon as I walked onto the court," he said. I recalled Jake's judgment; during a phone call one evening when we talked about Terrance, Jake had told me, "Ironically, Terrance was on the top on the outside, and in prison there's nothing higher than a cop killer." His cellmate then was a young man Terrance had known as a child when he lived in Southeast. He was a year or two older than Terrance and had been sentenced at sixteen to life imprisonment for murder.

"They say everything happens for a reason, and I figure this has to be for something that I did when I was younger," Terrance said, explaining his incarceration. "When I was fourteen, maybe fifteen, my mother caught me selling drugs, and she put me out. I went to live with her mother. And the deal for me to come back home was that I couldn't sell any more drugs. From that point on, I made a 3.0 grade average and started volunteering and was involved in sports, the Mayor's Youth Leadership Initiative, and the Male Youth Program."

He started selling drugs, he said, "to strike back at my mother's husband. I resented him a lot and felt jealous. I'd feel so bad, sometimes I didn't want to ask him for anything." So he began hanging out with older boys in the neighborhood, going to clubs where his prowess on the dance floor earned him large tips from the hustlers who liked just watching him move. They'd give him as much as fifty dollars sometimes just to dance.

"So when I'd get upset about things happening at home, the guys in the street would say, 'Don't worry about it,' " Terrance explained. The sequence of events Terrance narrated was ancient, predictable, yet still tragic. It was a story we all in some sense know, yet hope we will never have to hear about one of our own.

"And so one day I went with one of them and told them I wanted a package, and that's how it started." As Terrance sifted through a host of memories, I sat across from him watching an impressive display of his confidence, still resilient despite his conviction. I heard how articulate he was; I felt his energy and knew why Mike Statham had said, "He could've been a politician, a lawyer, a doctor, anything he wanted to be, he was that smart."

Over and over during our conversation, Terrance spoke of fights and his prowess with his hands. At the Male Youth Program, he told me, "They tried to get me into boxing because they had heard a lot about my hands." In his Southeast neighborhood he was known as a good fighter, and now he wondered aloud if some of the young men who befriended him saw him more as an enforcer than as someone they liked, as he said, "just because I was me."

And what did the fights mean to him? "It was just that I was young and I could fight well, and in the neighborhood fights, you always need somebody to fight for the way."

Yet Terrance insisted that he was a loyal, supportive friend "unless you rub me the wrong way. But if you give me one reason to believe that you're against me or something, you don't want to be my enemy. If I'm upset enough or you've done the wrong thing to me, there's no other way for me, you understand? If I'm mad enough to put my hands on you, there's no way I'm gonna walk away."

From behind prison bars, Terrance has forged a relationship with Albert Ross that is intimate and trusting. Ella had told me that when Terrance called home from prison, he asked to speak to his stepfather more often than to his mother. Ella said she knew that the two men had written letters to each other, letters she had not seen but that she suspected laid a foundation for the new bond they had forged.

"Why now?" I asked. "Why not before?"

"It's just that when I was home, my head was the size of this room," he said, moving reflexively to gesture with his handcuffed wrists to take in the room's small circumference. "You couldn't tell me anything because I thought I already knew it all. And we've had a chance to talk about all the things that should've been said before."

Of his biological father, Harry Dixon, Terrance said, "He's my father, and, yes, he's done drugs and sold drugs and been in and out of jail. What can I say? I guess he's got his reasons, but with me, he was always there. If he had the time, he spent it with me. When he found out I'd been selling drugs that time—he found out a long time after it happened—he told me things that maybe people would say a good father shouldn't, but he said, 'Look, it's too dangerous out there for you to be doing this. If you want to be doing something, you come to me and we'll work something out. If you mess somebody up and they end up dead, they're going to shut the door.'

"He approached the problem in his own way. He was my father, what can I tell you? When he was home after he had been released from jail, you couldn't keep me away from him. If he was home, I was gonna see him, stay up under him."

Of his mother, Terrance said, "She was strong enough to be a fine lineman. She taught me how to play football. How many people can say they got to the college level and their mother taught them that?"

I thought of Ella Ross, four feet eleven, maybe one hundred pounds. Seeing the surprise on my face, Terrance said, "She taught me how to put my finger on the strings and throw. She taught me how to catch, you know, to watch the ball and catch it, things of that nature. You don't have to be big to know the fundamentals."

• • •

I wondered if Terrance knew the real fundamentals his mother had taught and given him. I still did not know Terrance Brown when I left him that afternoon, but I knew what he had told me. His anecdotes, his observations, and his postures had created a picture of a youth who was, like many young men his age, conflicted about issues of power and identity. On the night of April 16, 1992, he was a young man who often settled disputes with violence. He loved his mother yet clearly yearned for the father he had not had, and he had not yet accepted the love Albert Ross extended. I wondered if Terrance Brown believed he deserved the promising future that had seemingly awaited him. Was there some part of him that saw himself not as Prime Time but as the son of a drug-dealing and -using father and the inheritor of a daunting level of sociological chaos and loss from the two families that had made him? Did Terrance Brown believe that despite the awards and the prizes, despite his mother's effort and the number of times she had beaten the odds, he was really a loser? Did that perhaps make it easier to endanger what he thought was not his by right to claim? Does a quick temper or choosing the wrong friends lead inevitably to robbery and murder? Legions of Black men in prison will tell you it can.

When I completed my interviews with Ella Ross and Terrance Brown, I talked with Michael about what I had discovered. A year had passed since Terrance's arrest. Michael had now had his own experience, albeit minor, with "the law." The average fourteen-year-old Black youth in Washington, DC, knows, as my son knew at the time of Terrance's arrest, of the reputation of the Prince Georges County police for being "tough on Black ass." If teens had not read about the numerous cases stretching back over two decades in which the Black community of Prince Georges County alleged excessive force or brutality, or in which Black suspects had been killed by the police under "unusual circumstances," then they had heard of these incidents from parents, relatives, or friends. Michael knew about the stories too. And because Terrance was initially placed in solitary confinement and there were rumors that Harry Mayo's damning testimony had been beaten out of him, Michael had at the beginning of Terrance's ordeal displayed the absolute conviction that Terrance was simply "set up."

I wondered how his views had changed in the intervening months. Was he still as certain as before that Terrance, like the man he had killed, was a victim?

So, one evening, I told Michael what I felt I knew, that Terrance, despite his outward confidence, was deeply troubled, and that, in a literal and figurative sense, he had been pulled by the competing values of the street and the straight life.

"Do you think he killed that guy on purpose?" Michael asked, stretching out on the sofa in my study.

"I don't know."

"If he hadn't had the gun," he said sadly, turning on his back to look at the ceiling. "He blew it."

"He said he was carrying the gun for protection," I said, deciding to play devil's advocate. "Remember when you were jumped by those boys near the subway and you were so angry you said you wished you had a gun, and if you did, you'd use it?"

"Yeah, but I was mad," he said, bolting upright in defense. "They shouldn't of jumped me. I didn't even know them."

"Maybe Terrance felt justified carrying a gun too."

"But he shot a cop. You know they'll never let him out. Not for killing a cop."

Terrance had ruefully predicted the same fate when I visited him.

"You know, when I was shoplifting that time, I knew it was wrong. But it was such a small thing, it didn't feel like a crime. Didn't you ever do something like that?"

Was I to tell him that when I was a college student, I routinely stole my required texts from the school bookstore? And that my friends and I had justified this act, calling it "liberation," not "theft," arguing that we were just reclaiming what "whitey" owed us anyway? I was never caught. So in the eyes of the law, I was innocent.

"Michael, it's your own soul, not mine, you're in charge of."

"I know you must've done something," he insisted, a mischievous gleam sparkling in his eyes, a smile crawling slowly across his face.

"You're my son, not my confessor. Now, come on and kiss me goodnight so you can get ready for bed. You still aren't too big to do that."

• • •

## JULY 10, 1993

Michael told me this evening that he has been having trouble sleeping at night as he thinks more and more about our trip. "Is it excitement or dread?" I asked. He said it was excitement.

## JULY 13, 1993

I talked today to Patrice Gaines, a friend and reporter for the Washington Post. She told me that last night her sixteen-year-old nephew was standing on a corner at Sixth and D Street SE with some friends talking when a young boy walked past them. A few minutes later, he walked back toward them and opened fire, shooting directly into their group. One young man was killed, one boy wounded; two others, including Patrice's nephew, were not hurt.

Is the callousness of some of the young murderers any greater than our indifference to their fates before they buy and then use a gun? Once they are certified criminals, we lose sleep fearing they will be housed in jails in our neighborhoods or set free on bond to kill again. Many of these young men are deemed expendable, so why should they not commit acts so heinous that they slit the throat of our complacency? If the luckiest ones, like the students I saw at Howard a few months ago, can be Black any way they choose, for the rest, our contempt has freed them to destroy us and themselves with a cunning that leaves us awestruck. There is a war on Black men, one waged externally—an objective analysis of the statistics on who goes to jail for certain crimes and who doesn't reveals that. But there is the internal war Black men wage against each other as well. How do you fight on two fronts?

## JULY 15, 1993

There was an article in the Post today concerning the shooting in which Patrice's nephew was involved. These were all just neighborhood boys, not drug dealers, standing on the corner on a summer night talking. One of the boys, Christopher Harvell, was a student of Joe's. He is a National Honor Society member who was class valedictorian at Dunbar this year and has been awarded a $100,000 scholarship from the Twenty-First Century Foundation to attend George Washington University, where he plans to study engineering. The dead youth, nineteen-year-old Henry Hank Lloyd, worked in a day-care center. Residents of the street say the youth who fired into the group feared they were rival drug dealers who planned to take over his corner.

## JULY 17, 1993

Earlier in the week, the churches in the city declared a seventy-two-hour moratorium against violence. There was extensive news coverage of the marches, rallies, and prayer meetings. How do you gauge the success of an effort like this? What does it mean that there were only three homicides during the moratorium, one a seventeen-year-old witness to the killing of a Howard University security guard? The boy was shot twenty times in broad daylight, his body discovered in an alley behind Wiltberger Street, not far from our house.

Where do reason and reality intervene in all of this? I read an article this evening arguing that if all youths—white, Asian, Black, Hispanic, Native American, et al., urban, suburban, and rural—are compared proportionately, there are more Latino gangs than Black gangs, and that white youths are victims of all forms of violence more than Black youths. But statistics can't measure pain or transcribe fear. And frankly, more Latino gangs, more dead white youths, do not reduce the number of dead Black males. I am jealously possessive of every life. I refuse to compute an acceptable ratio of dead Black boys to compare to that of dead white boys. Statistics are beholden to their manipulators for meaning; they are slippery, fickle, ultimately untrustworthy bits of perception that the pundits worship like some essential cosmic truth. The language statistics speak is imposed, not intrinsic. So each time I read another story padded with numbers, graphs, charts, creating a logarithm of human destruction, I know that what we are living in America in these days is a story that is fantastic, extraliterary, mundane, unbelievable, and thus, all the numbers are completely false and all the numbers are completely true.

Clyde McElvene says he feels that if the kids being killed in the cities were overwhelmingly white, there would be a massive national response to stop the violence. But do the powers that be really care about kids, white or Black? I told Clyde that maybe if the children of congresspersons or senators or industrialists and business magnates were being assassinated in the streets, maybe then there would be the kind of response he envisions. But if those being killed were just regular working-class, poor, or even middle-class white kids, I didn't think the response would be much different. This country has yet to decide to guarantee the health, the education, the safety, and the economic viability of all children, so the horrid bloody drama unfolding on the streets of the Black community is no more than an unashamed echo of the society's lethal indifference to the fate of all our kids. The longer white America turns away from the sight of the body bags piling up on our streets, the more it ensures that even behind the actual and psychological barriers it has erected, the corpses of their own young will begin to pile up too.

## JULY 19, 1993

I talked with Femi this morning. He said the atmosphere is still tense, but that while he can't guarantee anything, the worst of the demonstrations appear to be over. I keep trying to decide on an alternate time to make the trip. But there's no predicting that the situation will settle down anytime soon. I think I'm going to just act on faith and get on the plane.

## JULY 25, 1993

Bade and his family and my friend Louise met us at Kennedy to await the boarding of the plane to Nigeria. We'll be okay. I've decided that.

# Soon One Morning

The Lagos to which Michael and I returned was a city that offered stark evidence of Nigeria's social and economic decline. The worldwide economic downturn had transformed a city that was often intractable yet infused with an irresistible vitality into a town that was prostrate, nearly defeated. No longer the "official" capital of the country, Lagos remains, however, the only place where the educated can make a decent living, the hungry can find food, and the ambitious are able to make it big.

Upon our arrival at Muritala Mohamad International Airport, Michael and I were Zprocessed through customs quickly. As we approached the baggage claim area, I spotted Femi and his older brother Jide waiting in the anterior section. Both men were clearly elated when they saw me and then Michael. Soldiers, some with rifles slung casually over their shoulders, patrolled the arrival section as we waited twenty minutes for our bags to appear on the carousel. I stood wondering at how easy this moment felt, a moment I had fought for and yearned for so long. My son's father stood fifty feet away from us, and the thought, even as soldiers stalked the halls around me, made me feel somehow safer than I had in many years.

Femi and Jide greeted us with hugs, and Jide, who possessed an innate, nearly indelible air of authority and a deep-throated, yet seductive laugh, marveled at Michael's height.

Michael stood shyly before Femi, fumbling for a way to approach his father. Femi was more reserved than Jide. As father and former husband, he had feelings at that moment which, I knew, were deeper, more complex.

Jide and Femi had driven to the airport in separate cars, so Femi packed our bags in his trunk and took Michael in his car while I rode with Jide. Formerly an executive with Phillips Electronics, Jide informed me that he had now retired and was working as a consultant. We talked about the political situation in the country. Jide praised the presidential election as the most free and fair in the country's history. But the national currency, the naira, was virtually worthless, he said; inflation was phenomenal, and when I began to talk about economic problems in the United States, Jide quieted me with a blustering laugh, scolding me with the words, "If America is asleep, Nigeria is dead."

Bade proudly told me that Lagos had expanded in size in the fourteen years since I'd left. Indeed, the roads into the city were, as I remembered them, jammed, movement paralyzed by the infamous Lagos "go slow." I saw along the highways a few gleaming imported Japanese Toyotas and Subarus and sturdy Mercedes-Benzes, which maneuvered the often crater-filled dirt side Hondas, canary-yellow ramshackle taxicabs, and bruised, battered, fifteen-to-twenty-seat passenger buses called danfos, each filled to capacity, all of them spewing forth noxious fumes and carbon monoxide that formed a dark toxic cloud that squatted over the length and breadth of the city.

The ranks of the roadside peddlers of cookies, milk, fruits, newspapers, and even sandals and live chickens had been swelled by grown men and women, sometimes whole families. No longer was this a job just for young children and teenagers. I saw for the first time scores of beggars. Lagos, whose inhabitants are perhaps the hardiest, hardest-working souls on the planet (and who live and thrive in the face of water shortages, constant electricity outages, a crumbling infrastructure, and an unresponsive, inept governmental bureaucracy), had always been nonetheless a city where even the poorest could find something to sell, something to do to survive. But the beggars I saw along the roads informed me conclusively how much things had changed. And I realized, less than an hour back in the Third World, that these young men standing beside these awful roads, breathing in poisonous fumes all day, chasing mobile potential customers, and dodging the world's worst drivers were "endangered" too, though not by violence but by poverty.

Femi had his own private real estate company, housed in a small suite of offices in a section of Lagos called Palm Grove. At Femi's offices, we found Jide's wife, Bisi, and their son, Akinyinka, awaiting our arrival. Bisi had acted as my unofficial Nigerian surrogate mother, aiding my adjustment to customs and family politics as well as nursing me through the loss of my first child and the healthy birth of Michael. So our reunion was affectionate and heartfelt. Bisi teased Michael, telling him that she had taught me how to change his diapers and making him sit beside her so that she could just place her arms around his shoulders while we all sat and talked. Her son, Akinyinka, had been seven when I left the country. He was now a college student, pleased to see Michael and me, but deferential, respectful of me, in a manner unique to children raised in more traditional societies. We sat in Femi's office remembering the past, updating one another on the present. Shade, Bisi and Jide's daughter, was a student studying in London, and they showed me photos of her, a slender, beautifully coiffed and dressed young woman whose resemblance to her father was uncanny.

Soon Jide, Bisi, and Yinka departed, but before they left, Jide spoke for them all, I intuited, when he said to me as he looked again at Michael, tall, bright, and healthy, "Thank you for taking such good care of our son."

Michael wandered onto the balcony of Femi's office and stood talking with Leki, the brother of Femi's wife. Leki worked as Femi's messenger. Femi's secretary greeted me, saying, "Welcome, madam," with a slight bow, and I was thrust once again into the African caste system that I had never learned to accept fully. She was slight, attractive, her hair permed, her dress Western. Her deference to me was inspired by so much: I was a visitor, a guest, the former wife of her employer; I was an American, well educated, and a member of a higher "class" than she. Because of all this, from her perspective, real intimacy between us would be virtually impossible.

I watched Michael leaning on the iron banister with Leki, looking down on a street he had never seen before but watching it as though he had witnessed it every day of his life. And I heard the strains of the international language I soon learned connected young people around the world, making them a unique tribe of their own. The two stood talking animatedly about Michael Jordan, Michael Jackson, the rap group Naughty by Nature, Nike sneakers, Calvin Klein jeans.

Then Femi and I were alone in his office, and I wondered how to erase a decade of silence, hurt, and confusion. What did he feel at that moment? And because in our marriage it was always I who wanted to talk, to explain, to dissect and analyze, maybe too much, I took a deep breath and said simply, "Femi, I want to thank you for not dwelling on the past in your letters to me. I want to thank you for letting the past be just that."

"You were so afraid I would take Akintunde from you. You know I never meant those things I said."

"Femi, you only have to say the kinds of things you said once for them to be unforgettable, for them to hurt in a way that you think will never stop, for them to make you more afraid than you've been of anything before. You only have to say them once. You said them many more times than that."

"I never wanted to hurt you or Tunde. I never wanted to lose either of you."

"The letter I wrote you three years ago proves you didn't. Our presence here now does too."

And then we talked, about members of my family and close friends he remembered, and about his mother, now eighty-three, who had recovered from a long and deleterious bout with diabetes. Like everyone else in the country, he had been hit hard by the economic slump; still, he was building a house on the outskirts of Lagos and managing, he brooded gently, to keep "suffering and smiling," the Lagos motto for endurance in the face of adversity. In addition, he had been hospitalized for almost six months due to injuries suffered in a traffic accident, and he had lost money on some dubious investments. Femi was cynical, doubtful about the future of the country unless the President-elect was allowed to take office. As a businessman, he felt he could not leave Lagos, but the cost of living in the city, both financially and in terms of physical and emotional health, was staggering.

During our conversation, Michael entered the office and sat with us. As we talked, I savored this moment, the first time my son had seen me talking amicably with his father with no fear, no tension, in over a decade. It was a small moment, but one that contained the most valuable substance of all we would be given during this journey.

When we returned from lunch, Femi's wife, Ade, arrived, accompanied by Femi's four-year-old son, Akinyemi. Ade greeted me like an old friend, with an infectious smile for me and Michael. Our rapport was immediate as we talked about the resemblance between Michael and Akinyemi, the Nigeria Airways flight from New York, her job with the Education Ministry, mine at George Mason University. Yemi sat on the sofa sucking his thumb, quietly assessing Michael. He alternated a fascinated, studied watchfulness with the flickering beginnings of a smile as he warmed to his African-American brother. Michael led Yemi onto the balcony, where within moments Yemi was gleefully pummeling and punching Michael in a mock fight, yelling in his husky yet still childish voice, "I will beat you. I will beat you." English is the official language in Nigeria, the legacy of British colonialism; at his day-care center, Yemi learned English and Yoruba.

There came a moment when Ade, taking in the children, Femi, herself, and myself with a grand sweep of her arms, said, "I am glad we are happy together."

While Michael stayed with his father, I boarded with a cousin of one of Femi's oldest friends, Olu, who had been a kind of brother to me when Femi and I began dating. My host, Sola, was an administrator with the Lagos branch of an international bank. She made me feel entirely welcome in her home.

Michael spent most days with Femi at his office, watching him negotiate with clients or show various properties. One afternoon as Michael and I sat on the balcony of Femi's office, an older, richly robed man approached the building. Michael said, with a shake of his head, "My father won't be happy to see that man. He says he's trying to cheat him, and he can't get away with that. I've watched my father work: He drives a hard bargain, he knows how to get what he wants."

Michael quickly became friends with a boy a year younger than himself who lived next door to Femi's office. My son greeted his father's friends with the required humble bow of the head and in awkward but sincere Yoruba, which I had taught him before our departure: "Ekuarro" ("Good morning"), "Odabo" ("Goodbye"). English was usually spoken in his presence, Yoruba if the conversation was confidential or private. When I, who had lived in Lagos for four years, complained of the relentless, endless snarl of traffic, the sporadic flow of electricity, Michael told me impatiently, "Mom, we're only gonna be here two weeks. You act like it's forever."

After witnessing Ade killing and plucking a live chicken for dinner one night, Michael became obsessed with the desire to kill a chicken on his own. One afternoon we went to the market with Ade. As we got out of the car, Ade winked at me and said in a serious, nearly ominous voice to Michael, "You want to kill a chicken, today you can kill a chicken. I will see to that."

The market was a series of twisting passageways lined with stalls selling anything that could be grown, made, or imported, legally or illegally. The market women, who had been at their posts since early morning, were as savvy as traders in oil or diamonds. As we passed the stalls, which curled in a seemingly endless labyrinth, the women called out, "Customer, customer." But Ade knew exactly where she was going, and we finally arrived at a spacious wooden stall filled from floor to ceiling with caged fowl. She told the owner in Yoruba that she wanted to buy a chicken. Then she grabbed Michael by the hand and together they inspected the caged birds. Michael pointed to several chickens. Ade and the owner haggled over size and price as Michael smiled at me, so excited he could barely stand still. I stood lagging behind them, amazed by this, to my mind, bloodthirsty display of aggression by my son. Was he merely going to assist Ade with dinner in this exercise, or was this desire symbolic of the serial killer lurking inside? I stood trying to remember that in two hours we would be feasting on whatever bird Michael chose and that then motivation wouldn't much matter.

Finally the bird was chosen and the owner's helper reached in and grabbed the squalling, healthy, white-feathered fowl by the neck. Ade paid for the bird. Michael was handed a machete and the bird was placed on the cement floor. Ade crouched on her knees holding the legs; the young helper held the head. Michael almost gleefully decapitated the chicken in two swift blows. The deed done, Michael danced proudly around the stall.

One evening a beggar ran up to the car window, his hand outstretched. The man hobbled on a makeshift cane fashioned from a stick and directed his gaze at Ade and then at me, but it was Michael who pleaded for coins to give him. Michael placed the coins in the man's hand with a solemnity and purpose that astonished me. Seeing this, Ade turned to me and said, "You took him away, but his soul remained here. He is an African."

Nigeria was in the throes of a religious boom. One day as Ade and I talked about the hundreds of churches that had sprung up all over Lagos, she told me, "Times are so hard now, and people feel, if you can't have bread, at least you can have God." Billboards lined the major and minor roads; fliers and posters seemingly filled every inch of public space advertising congregations like the Faith Family Church, the poster illustrated with a drawing of a contented family gazing heavenward. Evangelists aired televised services.

The evening news was tightly controlled by the military government, and each evening at Sola's, I watched the melodramatic, tragic accounts, which were really undisguised propaganda urging the country to remain calm, not to take to the streets once again. I sat depressed and uncertain each evening, watching footage of delegations of politicians, from all the political parties and from around the country, meeting with Babangida, who vainly attempted to appear to be a statesman rather than a thief. Numerous newspapers and magazines had been seized and shut down, their editors and journalists thrown in jail for any act or word deemed critical of the government. Femi refused to read The Daily Times, now considered a mere mouthpiece for the military government that refused to step down. In Femi's office each afternoon, the talk was as much of the fate of the country as of business.

One afternoon, Michael, Yemi, Yinka, and I went on an excursion to Lekke Beach, located on Victoria Island, an exclusive preserve where diplomats, wealthy foreigners, and many affluent Nigerian businessmen owned spacious apartments and homes.

Femi's driver took us into the city. The traffic in Lagos is a hydra-headed monster, and even in the midst of a gasoline shortage in this oil-producing country that had motorists waiting hours in line for petrol and had decreased the number of cars on the roads, the traffic remained a test of ingenuity, strength, and will. There were no driving schools in Lagos, and so on the roads and behind the wheel, improvisation most often reigned. On the bridge leading to Lagos Island, the commercial heart of the city, we passed an accident. The two drivers, one a burly danfo driver whose facial tribal marks unfurled like foliage on his cheeks, and the other a well-dressed driver of an Acura Legend whose suit I had seen in the window of Hugo Boss in Washington's fashionable Georgetown shopping district, stood raining curses upon one another. The front of the Legend was dented, and the owner gazed at the car as if assessing the broken body of a family member. The two men were, as we snaked by them, in the midst of a furious bout of posturing, one that allowed them to approach one another within a few feet, make a series of insulting, metaphorically lethal gestures with arms and hands, and curse and slander one another, all while being reined in by the crowd that had gathered around them.

I knew that someone in the crowd would mediate a face-saving way for each man to leave the scene with some measure of dignity intact. A foul curse upon one's house or family was as lethal as these altercations got. The thought that a private citizen would reach into a car trunk or beneath a car seat and pull out a gun to close the matter was inconceivable.

In the back seat, as we neared the beach, Michael and Yinka sat discussing the film *Boyz N the Hood,* which Yinka had seen on video. (Nearly every middle-class home I had entered since our arrival had a VCR.) Despite the seven-year age difference, the two talked animatedly and shared numerous interests. Listening to them, I remembered Michael's question, "What would I be like if I had grown up in Nigeria?" Bisi and I had talked about our sons. When Yinka was fourteen, she sent him to a private boarding school in Ondo State for reasons similar to those that had made me choose Westtown as an option and opportunity for Michael. "Oh, he was silly, and immature, playful. I felt he really needed to be away from us," she explained with a laugh. "By the time he graduated, you know, they had straightened him out."

But I knew that my son, had he come of age in Nigeria, would have been less individualistic, more conscious of and influenced by family, community, tribe. I knew, too, that he would have taken his racial identity for granted as a reality, neither positive nor negative, in a way that was impossible in the highly charged, insidiously racial atmosphere of America.

At twenty-two, Yinka had only one more year of undergraduate studies to complete before graduating. But for the past three years, the military government had closed colleges and universities throughout the country in labor disputes with faculty over pay, and many felt it had been done to neutralize the political influence of students, often the first to demonstrate and rally against government policy.

As Shade was her father's daughter, Yinka was his mother's son, possessing her long, angular, open face even while he had his father's height. When we arrived at the beach, Michael and Yinka swam for several hours while Yemi and I collected seashells. Then, over a lunch of barbecued meat, I asked Yinka about his studies at the University of Lagos, where I had once taught. Three months before our arrival, the government had closed the university, effectively canceling the remainder of the term. Yinka was an English major but said that ultimately he wanted to study law or international relations at the graduate level. When I asked him what I had asked Marc, if there was anything that he feared when he thought about the future, he said, "I'm afraid I won't be able to be someone who can raise and take care of a family, someone whom others can depend on, not someone depending on anyone else." The stagnant economy had turned the search for employment Yinka had launched since the university shutdown into a futile, cruel joke.

More than anything, he told me, he longed for money and a passport to go to England to join his sister Shade. "At least there, the universities wouldn't be closed, I could finish my education, get my degree."

As I listened to the sincerity and frustration in my young relative's voice, I thought of the violent climate of racial intolerance then infecting England and so much of Europe, which had made cities like London, Paris, and Berlin, once hallowed in the minds of former colonials, dangerous places for "colored" men and women. And even more unjust, I felt, was that twenty years after Jide had journeyed abroad to study, idealistically hoping to return and build a viable nation, Nigeria could neither absorb his son's considerable talents in the job market nor guarantee him a seat in the university. Yinka's plight mirrored the bitter, unfinished legacy my generation had bequeathed our sons and daughters in the generation after the civil rights struggle. I was learning every day how slippery and relative concepts like "safety" or "progress" could be in these days of global interdependence, with the Third World tottering beneath the weight of a "new world order" more exploitative, racist, and dangerous than the old one. Everywhere I looked, my people were plugging holes in the same rickety boat.

• • •

How to determine the quality and quantity of affection and trust that Michael and Femi shared, found, built? I watched Femi with Yemi, who, at four, had a Herculean temper, yet who was engaging and curious and saw a parent at once indulgent and firm. What kind of father would he have been to Michael? I vaguely recalled that in the first year of Michael's life, he was a proud father, protective of his son, unwilling to deny him anything. I spent two evenings with Femi and Ade and saw that the initial awkwardness between Femi and Michael has dissolved—without me. Already Michael had learned how far he could go in negotiating favorable terms for his requests, and Femi attempted to balance the imposition of boundaries and limits with indulgence, perhaps to make up for all the lost time. They watched televised soccer together, played marathon games of Monopoly. A thousand small verbal exchanges, facial expressions, mundane conversations, jokes, irritations, moments of laughter, political debates, untruths, and inquisitions created something between them that Michael could not, when I asked him, explain, but only possess.

I had awaited this journey with greater anticipation, I felt, than even Michael, and so I was eager in the midst of it to gain a sense of what was transpiring between father and son, how they found the way, each day, to one another. When I asked Michael one afternoon how he and Femi were getting along, he told me, "You know, my father doesn't really talk a lot. He asks the kind of questions you ask somebody you don't know."

"That's to be expected."

"He asks what I like to do, what I want to study in college, what I'd like to be when I grow up."

"Do you feel distant from him?"

"Not distant, but I feel closer to Yemi and Yinka."

"He loves you. I hope you can see that, even though it's hard for him to express it."

As we talked, I thought of the way Femi possessively threw his arm around Michael when they sat in the back seat of the car together. I knew that displays of affection were difficult for him. That arm casually slung over our son's shoulder, and the look on Femi's face that articulated a subtle, hard-won contentment, reveling quietly in the moment, spoke what Michael was too young to hear or understand.

And Michael had not been privy to my conversation with Femi in which he told me, "Things are terrible in the country right now. But by the time Akintunde is ready for college, he could come here for a year or so and it wouldn't be as expensive as in the States." I thought of the closed university campuses but also of the young woman we had met at Kennedy Airport the evening of our departure. Her father was Yoruba and her mother was African American. She was twenty years old and told us that after her parents divorced when she was five, she remained in Nigeria with her father for several years, then came to the United States to live with her mother. With her cornrowed hair, her bubbly charm, and the ease with which she spoke Yoruba, the young woman was impressive. She lived a transatlantic life, shuttling between Nigeria and the United States easily, and she had studied for a time at the University of Lagos before it was closed by the government. I looked at the young woman and hoped Michael would one day fit as easily as she in both the homes he could legitimately claim.

And there was often a softness, a gentleness, in Femi's voice as he spoke to Michael. His pride was evident when he introduced him to friends or associates, who were amazed at Michael's height and how much he resembled Femi. "This is my son, who lives in America with his mother," he'd say.

There was the list Michael was compiling of items to bring to Nigeria to sell when he came back to visit again—tapes, clothing, watches. He asked me to help him make purchases for such a trip. Femi had promised to help him sell whatever he brought. This entrepreneurial zeal was Femi's imprint, not mine.

Michael had returned to Nigeria to claim his status as "older son" in Femi's house. He was part oyingbo, "foreigner," but he was also blood and the firstborn male child. And so Femi indulged him, scolded him, but gently, when required, and had Ade prepare fried chicken, french fries, salad, and other American dishes to accommodate Michael's palate. Femi did all this not because Michael was a guest but because he was his boy-child.

And so I told Michael, "It will take time to build the closeness. I just wanted you to know your father and that he is here for you."

"I'm glad we came. And I want to come back. I'm glad I've seen my father. I have friends who never did. Their dads died when they were real young, or they walked out on the family. At least I got to see my father and know who he is."

Femi and Michael were separated as much by the passage of time as by culture. For the intense conversations that Michael often shared with Joe, during which they discussed sports and politics and life almost as equals, were absent in Nigeria. Michael's opinion was unsought by his father or the Ajayi clan, even while they loved him and celebrated his return. The lines of demarcation between parent and child were bolder in this society that as stranger and inheritor my son sought to claim.

• • •

Several days before our departure, Femi, Jide, Michael, and I drove to Femi's hometown, Ado Ekiti, to visit his mother. We arrived in the town near dusk after a five-hour drive from Lagos. Our first stop was at a large, many-roomed house owned by Jide and used by family members visiting Ado Ekiti, for Femi's mother had little space in her house for visitors.

Femi's mother was Michael's only living grandparent. She was the only person in whose face he could see what elements of biology and character spawned one of his parents. She was the only living thread my son had to the genesis of what and who created him.

There was electricity in the town now and the major road leading into Ado Ekiti was paved. But there had been no water running through the town's pipes for the past four days, and driving in the early evening dusk to Femi's mother's house, we passed young girls and boys, men and women, carrying buckets of water retrieved from the town's main pump. Progress had arrived, I was told, but Ado Ekiti remained a town mostly of goats, old people, and small children. Years before, when I had visited Femi's mother for the first time, a goat was slaughtered in celebration. But inflation had made such a feast impossible to consider for Michael's return, and we stopped several times during the drive to buy yams, fruit, and bread for Femi's mother, for hunger had returned to many parts of the country outside the large cities.

"Mama," as I had always called Femi's mother, stood in her tiny parlor awaiting our arrival. Despite her battle with diabetes, the only change was the color of her cornrowed hair, now almost solidly white. One of eight wives, a devout Christian who honored both the Western God and her traditional tribal beliefs, she urged Femi and Jide to take only one wife. Once she told me that now that I was an Ajayi, she finally had a daughter. I laughed, suspecting that she had told Bisi, Jide's wife, this as well. But that did not matter, for her loyalty was inclusive and resilient.

She was the only person whom Femi truly feared and respected, the only person in the family whose will he would, in moments of anger, submit to without question.

The tiny brown eyes embedded in her amazingly unlined face were luminous when she spotted Michael striding into the room behind Femi. She clapped her hands, gazed skyward, and mouthed a prayer in Yoruba, thanking God for our return. As required, Michael, all five feet eight of him, prostrated himself before his grandmother as a sign of respect, and she smiled broadly in satisfaction and pleasure. My son had, according to his father's tradition, merely given the woman to whom he in some measure owed his life a small part of her due.

Mama shared her house with almost a dozen people who rented rooms from her. And so, small children with huge searching eyes and distended bellies; young girls, giggling and surprised by the sight of my son, tall, wearing braces, speaking a language they only partially understood; and young women who helped care for Mama and who had been told that her grandson was coming from America—all stood on the edges of the room, witnesses to our reunion.

Femi translated for me, for his mother spoke no English. Michael gave her the strand of pearls we brought as a token, and, as she placed them around her neck, he told a young woman to bring her a mirror. Satisfied with what she saw in the mirror, she then paraded around the small room cocking her head in a merry display, to the delight of all gathered. I had given Femi three hundred dollars for his mother, which he had sent to her via a friend days before our arrival, and she thanked me for the money.

Once again she launched into prayer, this time urging us all onto our knees. After the prayer, she gazed at me with a mischievous yet determined look in her eye and asked through Femi if I would stay this time. I told her that I had a husband back in the States to whom I must return. She accepted my answer but assured me that I remained her daughter nonetheless.

As Femi and his mother talked, through the small window I heard a small radio perched between two men sitting outside, and on it the sound of a French radio station. Femi told me that among the people who now lived with his mother were immigrants from Mali who had fled that country because of the drought.

Michael sat in our midst, fidgeting, bored. After a while, he asked if he could go outside to sit on the front porch. Femi and I said that he could.

As Femi and I prepared to return to the guest house, we went outside to find Michael in animated conversation with several young women and men. In the darkness, Michael sat on the small cement stoop, encircled by a group of young girls and women, who sat rapt, listening to him talk. Femi laughed and told me that he was certain that because of Michael's accent, those gathered understood perhaps only half of what he said. But clearly they were enthralled by his height, his strong, aggressive presence, and the way he used space and his body.

"Tomorrow they will brag that they met an oyingbo," Femi said.

Michael begged to stay there for the night. "At least there's someone here to talk to," he explained. "Back there it's just you adults."

The next morning, when we drove back to Mama's house to get Michael, he told us that he had slept with his grandmother because there was no extra bed. I recalled that on my first visit I had shared a bed with Mama too, while Femi slept in his father's house. My rest had been calm and unperturbed. Michael said mosquitoes kept him awake all night. When I asked how he communicated with Mama, Michael shrugged, saying simply, "We figured it out." Then I took pictures of Femi, Mama, and Michael together, gave small monetary tokens to several elders who lived nearby, and with hugs and promises, we said goodbye.

On the way out of the town, Femi showed Michael several plots of land that he had inherited on his father's death, land formerly used as part of his father's rubber plantation.

"I'm going to retire here," he said.

"You'll never retire," I teased him. "You'll never leave Lagos."

"Yes I will."

"I want to live to see it."

"So do I." He smiled.

"Because this land is mine, it's also yours," Femi told Michael, staring at him in the rearview mirror. "I will see to that."

I settled back in my seat in the front watching Ado Ekiti pass by and thought that maybe as much as Michael had come back to find his father, he had returned as well to claim another "place" that could be his. He had found a father, cousins, aunts, uncles—and land, untilled, lying fallow, but his one day, on which he could make something grow.

• • •

Shortly after our return from Nigeria, we moved to Mitchellville, Maryland. In mid-September, Michael entered Westtown. I learned quite soon that Michael had not merely been "sent away" to school but had become part of an academic, cultural, and social community that would have potentially enormous impact on him.

I missed him intensely the first several weeks, but gradually came to appreciate the peace of mind that came with knowing he was in a safe environment. The school year in Washington had opened on a violent note when, on the second day of classes, a junior high school student sprayed random gunfire into a group of other students walking to a bus stop.

At Westtown, Michael, always socially adept, quickly made friends. But his mid-term grades the first semester were dismal. And shortly after Thanksgiving, I received a call from the school psychologist, who told me several of Michael's teachers had begun to suspect that his poor performance was an indication of attention deficit disorder. In response, she had conducted a series of tests with Michael that indicated he might indeed suffer from ADD, but a more formal diagnosis was still needed. The school psychologist phoned one day before I had planned to restart the diagnostic process at the National Institutes of Health with a call to Dr. Zametkin.

By the time he came home for Christmas, Michael knew that his difficulties in consistently achieving up to his potential might be neurologically based. But he was angry and confused, and thought that the results of the tests the school psychologist had given him meant he was retarded. A few days before Christmas, Dr. Peter Jensen, an associate of Dr. Zametkin's at NIH, talked at length with Michael and with Joe and me about Michael's problems in paying attention and completing tasks both at home and at school. He also assessed the test results from Westtown and the reports of Michael's teachers. Dr. Jensen diagnosed Michael as suffering from ADD. Because Michael was not hyperactive, it had been very difficult to recognize the signs of ADD earlier. Dr. Jensen told us that like many of those with the disorder, Michael was very bright and articulate and could focus intensely on subjects that interested him. His attention span was fractured, however, when it came to assigned tasks.

On Christmas Eve, I took Michael to see Audrey Chapman, for I was worried about his continuing inability to accept the fact that he had a learning difference and about his fear that it meant he was mentally handicapped. Michael talked with Chapman in detail about his fears, his anxieties, his questions. Perhaps because he had confided in her before, after talking with him for an hour, she was able to convince him to work with the staff at Westtown, with his doctor, and with Joe and me to develop a treatment strategy.

From the sessions with Dr. Jensen and Audrey Chapman, I learned for the first time that Michael often simply "phased out" in the middle of classroom lectures, that he would frequently begin a project and simply be unable to continue to focus. Michael had never told me any of this. He did not know how.

I felt tremendous relief, for I felt that I finally knew why there had been such a wide and continuing gap between Michael's potential and his achievement. The treatment strategy consisted of medication, as well as special tutoring tailored to his learning style and designed to help him develop techniques that would enable him to stay on task and become more organized. I had been told by the school psychologist that there were numerous students at Westtown who had ADD and who performed well academically.

In my need to help Michael cope with the implications of the diagnosis, I read several books on attention deficit disorder. One book, written by a respected educational psychologist, asserted that nearly all American schoolchildren suffered unprecedented levels of inattention, lack of focus, and poor concentration. The pervasive influence of television and video games and the radical changes in family cohesion and parenting styles had produced, this author argued, a generation of youngsters whose thought patterns were fuzzy and incomplete and who had difficulty digesting any idea that couldn't be grasped in thirty seconds.

But the more I read about ADD, the more conflicting seemed the evidence of its prevalence. The diagnostic process had relied heavily on anecdotal summaries from Michael, his teachers, and Joe and me. Why, I began to wonder, were middle- and upper-class children disproportionately diagnosed as having learning disabilities? Did the goal-oriented, achievement-conscious values of upscale families encourage labeling of any child who failed early on to achieve high grades? The evidence seemed to support this conclusion. Why was it so frequently recommended that boys essentially be medicated in the classroom? A pediatrician friend warned me, explaining, "ADD has become the fashionable diagnosis. It's overdiagnosed and is used to explain a myriad of connected and disconnected behavior and learning problems."

After months of reading, researching, and talking with parents whose children had been diagnosed with various learning differences, I concluded that I simply did not know for sure whether Michael suffered from ADD—that really, nobody knew.

I did know that, at sixteen, my son had a pattern of problems in sustaining focus and attention academically. In public school, Michael had typically played his way through the first half of the year, and then, fearing summer school or failure, had made average to good grades in the final semester. Did Michael have ADD, or was he just lazy? Did he require intense pressure to perform well at tasks he wasn't drawn to? Even his admission that he "phased out" in class was not necessarily definitive, at least not to me. Was he unable to be attentive, or was he easily distracted? Did he choose not to concentrate? I began to wonder if maybe my son's public school teachers' conclusion that "he just hasn't learned to buckle down," or their conjecture that "he'll grow out of it," might not be just as valid as Dr. Jensen telling Joe and me that, with the passage of adolescence, the symptoms of ADD subside in some children and they can learn to compensate for their learning problems without the use of drugs.

By the end of the first year at Westtown, Michael had raised his grades, although they remained marginal. He remained sporadically disorganized and often inconsistent in his approach to studying, but he spoke more often than in the past of really wanting to do well academically. He began talking about college and careers he was considering. Michael was growing up, struggling to meet the expectations of parents and teachers, as well as suddenly new expectations of himself, which he had perhaps been afraid to impose before. The academic rigors of Westtown had challenged him, and he admitted more than once that he felt "special" as a member of the Westtown community.

During this first year, Michael had battled with fears that he was academically out of his league, had read Zora Neale Hurston's *Their Eyes Were Watching God*, had shone in his theater class, had learned to grasp equations in algebra, had been a member of the basketball and baseball teams, had run for the post of prefect on his floor, and had counted as one of his best friends at the school a young man from Malaysia. I had stayed in touch regularly with his advisors and counselors, his tutor and teachers, attempting to monitor his progress while not making him feel burdened by my intrusions. Michael was literally surrounded by a human safety net of adults, all of whom worked with and came to know him intimately, and who like me pushed and encouraged him to do nothing less than his best.

I now felt ready to work with him more on consciously building his confidence and self-esteem, modifying his behavioral patterns and his attitude toward responsibility, and relying a little less on the medication. The diagnostic process had given me crucial information about my son that I might not have discovered any other way. And using this information, I was learning what systems of rewards and punishments, what types of motivation and encouragement, worked best with Michael. As his parent, it was my responsibility to combine a close reading of the child I still knew better than any doctor with a critical assessment of the treatment prescribed for whatever medical problems he was deemed to possess. Because Michael tended in his behavior often to take shortcuts, I felt that reliance on medication transmitted exactly the opposite message a child with his inclinations should receive.

In one year, my son had been reunited with his father, had left home to attend boarding school, and had had thrust upon him an unsettling, unfamiliar assessment of his abilities. Michael was still learning how emotionally strong he could be. He remained, then, a child, an adolescent, stumbling yet guided by the map made by those who loved him toward an adulthood he could not fathom but only fiercely desire.

I do not know what choices my son will make, what type of life he will live, what he will choose to believe, how he will use his talents. I do know that he was, and is, loved. I know that he has seen those who cared about him reach always for the highest and brightest star. I only wish for Michael his own galaxy and the determination to reach for it himself.

# Epilogue

Every sentence is a search for truth. Each paragraph is a window; each page, an open door. I wrote about sons because at this moment there is no subject more necessary to confront, more imperative to imagine. Until I wrote about our sons, I could not speak or think or dream of anything else.

The specter of death, real, unexpected, and cruel, has filled these pages. Death, like some medieval plague, is now with us. And if we love our sons and our daughters and ourselves, we must speak death's name, step up to it, challenge it, fight it collectively and one-on-one.

But an insatiable desire for, and commitment to, life has fueled these words. We bury and mourn the sons who are dead. What will we do to cherish and save the ones who live?

If the daily transgressions against safety, sanity, and well-being that prevail in pockets of the Black community were committed against us by members of any other race, these acts would be labeled terrorism. How else to describe a group of boys on a street corner forcing a young man at gunpoint to first hand over his coat and then strip naked? Clothes were stolen, but dignity was appropriated as well. Standing outside my husband's school at dusk that evening, perhaps hoping as he disrobed that a police car might happen by, the young man probably mumbled what he thought would be his last prayer ever. For he had grown up in the neighborhood, was on his way to an after-school job. He knew that the slightest glimmer of insolence, rebellion, or anger reflected in his voice or eyes could inspire a finger to press the trigger.

In the opening pages, I metaphorically claimed both the young man standing naked on a nighttime street corner and the boys who sped off with his clothes as my sons. What else was I to do? So I urge us to tell our sons every day, over dinner, in the bathroom, in school, on the basketball court, on the phone, during the commercial break, in Sunday school, before they go to bed, when they get up, when they head off to college, when they come home, when we visit them in jail, when we attend their weddings, when we mourn at the funerals of their friends: You have a choice, you are responsible for what you do, and your community will hold you accountable. Racism will never change that. Long after our eyes glaze over and our ears grow numb watching and listening to the TV roundtable discussions that seek to address our fate, we can still keep our sons awake and perhaps alive if we teach them that the first line of defense against racism is to mold themselves into disciplined, self-respecting refutations of its ability to destroy our souls or ourselves. This is not a platitude. And telling our sons they can make a choice and not have life merely happen to them does not render the choices always palatable or benign.

Of course, in the most ultimate, far-reaching sense, it is only the dismantling of institutional racism that will guarantee the lives of our sons and all our children. All the most objective and uniformly respected studies have found, year after year, that my son, prep school-educated and world-traveled, will nevertheless be discriminated against in every endeavor of his life, from hailing a taxi to applying for a job or a mortgage to buying a car. Michael, like all of America's Black sons, pays a "Black tax" on his existence every day of his life. I am anguished and angry confronting that reality. Our sons are too.

The lives and legacy of African Americans have been progressive and valuable beyond measure simply because each generation has fashioned a way to resist the pernicious hold of racism on our lives. My son's generation is the first that may be destroyed before it can marshal its forces against the enemy arrayed at the border. The battle this time is even bloodier, the lines more deeply drawn.

And yet this examination of my life and my son's life has revealed answers embedded in the minutiae of my struggle to make it through each day, answers I fashioned unknowingly, with fingers crossed in the dark, afraid I'd never see the light: answers that I found because I was more afraid not to seek them out than I was of what they might be.

African-American women must forgive the real and imagined crimes of their sons' fathers. We must resist the urge to visit upon all the men in our lives the bitterness and pain planted by incompetent fathers or disappointing lovers. Forgiving Michael's father was the most important, difficult action I have taken in my role as mother. There is nothing else that I have done for my son that approaches that step in importance.

Forgiving my son's father did not transform my ex-husband, but it did allow Michael to see the best in me, and it paved a path for him to cross to reach the man who gave him life. Our sons need their fathers, even when they are absent; they need to know who they are so that they can confirm their own identity. The generations-old backlog of anger that African-American men and women hoard, revisit, and, with a genius that is frightening, unleash upon one another becomes a script that our sons and our daughters memorize, practicing its lethal intent and perfecting it in their own lives.

We Black women must forgive Black men for not protecting us against slavery, racism, white men, our confusion, their doubts. And Black men must forgive Black women for our own sometimes dubious choices, divided loyalties, and lack of belief in their possibilities. Only when our sons and our daughters know that forgiveness is real, existent, and that those who love them practice it, can they form bonds as men and women that really can save and change our community.

In the absence of traditional family structures, we can and must recreate the meaning of family. That was formerly one particular genius of African Americans. Every Black church in America should adopt and become responsible for the sons of its racial community as well as the sons of its congregation.

There was a transcendent moment in our history when we faced bulldogs, water cannons, jail cells, firebombs, assassinations, and sacrifice so that our children could be full citizens. What will we do so that they can live? We have faced guns before. In the past they were aimed at us by mobs cloaked in white sheets, but never held on us by our own sons. Do we now fear our children more than we feared racists? Did we want to integrate more than we now want to save ourselves from extinction?

We know what is required, a moral and ethical transformation that will make us both bold and compassionate, intuitive and strategic, demanding and forgiving. We created and became our best selves in the "struggle for freedom." Why do we resist the same call to deliver our young? The chaos that reigns in pockets of the Black community today is as arbitrary, complicated, and fearsome as the brutality of the undeclared guerrilla war that Southerners unleashed to preserve segregation.

We know how to win moral and material skirmishes, how to create an army of domestic workers, college students, janitors, and preachers. We know how to march and shame a nation. Our failure to push ourselves past the net of the conventional, the safe, shames us now. The present challenge descends directly from the partial answers, the unfinished business, that Black and white America left behind in a rush toward self-congratulation. Paralyzed by debate, indifferent, factionalized, unable to caucus unless the cameras wait outside the door, we watch as our sons meanwhile embrace destruction. We will not place ourselves between them and the madness because we don't love them enough to insist, to demand, to require that they live.

## NOVEMBER 10, 1993

Joe came home from school today and handed me the following note which he had written during his lunch break:

Marita, I feel the need to write and communicate with God. People like you grab your pen and write out your problems or write through them. But today I was faced with something I had feared for some time. During the 1985-86 school year, I met a teacher who had lost one of her students to violence. Two Black males took the student's boom box and blew him away. I felt so sorry for that teacher that I prayed for the child, for his parents, and for the teacher. In the years since then, I have prayed as well for students, former students, just that they would be safe, that they would survive. But today it happened, what I had been afraid of. I wonder. Only God knows. A student in my homeroom has contracted AIDS. Do we have to literally step over our children's dead bodies? When will it end?

Love, Joe.

Marc decided a year after taking my class at Antioch that he indeed did want to pursue a career as a writer. He won an honorable mention in a national competition for African-American college writers, the Zora Neale Hurston/Richard Wright Award. His story "Mercury" was awarded third place out of forty-seven submissions from all over the country. Marc decided to study creative writing at the graduate level after he graduated from Antioch. Today Marc is an award-winning novelist, artist, and professor of creative writing at the University of Pennsylvania.

Terrance Brown took college courses offered at the Lorton Correctional Complex by Coppin State College and made the dean's list and the honor roll. His name was submitted to the National Dean's List directory for inclusion in the 1994–95 edition. Terrance died while incarcerated.

Michael entered the eleventh grade at Westtown in the fall of 1994 and for the first time in years began the academic year confident and achieving good grades. He admitted that in his first year at Westtown he was girl crazy and had not studied. At sixteen, going on seventeen, he was suddenly obsessed with making good grades and getting into a good college. Today, Michael is a social media influencer. His wife is a professor of political science and they have a year-old daughter.

# The Dead Call Us to Remember

Below are some of the men who have died violently in Washington, DC, since 1988. They were killed during arguments, robberies, drug deals, while at play, sitting in cars, standing on corners, in their homes, walking home from work, in alleys, and on playgrounds. They were thirteen, forty-two, seventy-four, and their deaths were caused by knife stabs, beatings, and gunshots. Some were shot as they sat in cars, others were shot from passing cars. They died at midnight, in the middle of the day. They were barbers, mechanics, owners of their own businesses, rap musicians, white-collar workers, gang members and schoolboys and fathers and husbands and sons.

| | |
|---|---|
| Kevin Darnell | William A. Best |
| Louis W. Gelman | Frederick Glenn |
| Donnie Michaels | Julian Timberlake |
| Christophe Jones | Darnell Wells |
| Ernest P. McQueen | Habib Mathis |
| Floyd Payne | Anthony F. Bailey |
| Terrance Sealey | Derrick W. Bell |
| Joseph T. Sams | Richard Lewis Clark |
| Michael R. Robinson | Cecil R. Curry |
| Linden S. Ault | Carlton Earl Dickens |
| Thomas Brown, Jr. | Derrick Chase |
| Eric N. Butler | Gary Hickman |
| Bob Gerald Trever | Leonard Allen Morrison |
| Jamie Banker | Cedric M. Johnson III |
| Raymond Campbell | Jimmy Blade |
| Raymond C. Davidson | Anthony E. Wright |
| Eugene M. Artis | Wesley S. Gorham |
| Demitrius Coleman | James A. Mingo |
| David Williams | Darryl Johnson |
| Maurice W. Crutchfield | Willard E. Jones |
| William C. Johnson | Larry A. Rawles |

Thomas W. Moore
Robert Lee Hill
Anthony L. Slappy
Paul A. Frazier
Norman R. Oakcrum
Julio Perryman
Reginald K. Peters
William Craig Haley
Norman Brown
Mawu Robinson
Cassius C. Keys
Anthony T. Tate
Vernon A. Mitchell
Steven West
Michael Olds
Robert E. Lewis
Keith Mayo
Kenneth Jones
Kevin A. Clements
Christopher Conley
Lawrence Monroe
Franklin Smith
Lonnie O. Hutchinson
Warren Harris
Ronald K. Thompson
Lee Oliver Williams
Donald Bolton
Zachery J. Ray
Julius Robinson
Eddie Nell Martin
Tachious J. Owens
Reginald Lewis
Reginald Duckett
James Harris Brooks
Warren Morgan
Stanley McCrae
Cory Hines
Steven L. Parker

Emory Lewis Trawick
Lonnie Hart, Jr.
Albert Thomas
Reginald Walker
Steven Maxwell
Alvin Winstock
Daryl W. Murchison
David Lewis Hodge
Anthony Paul Hestop
Melvin Douglas Brown
Michael McCurdy
Samuel A. Mack
Kevin Eans
William A. Wilson
Larry McCaspling
Wade Malone
Johnnie Lee Green
Victor O. Tatum
Albert E. Webb
Bobby Workman
Charles Brandon, Jr.
Kevin A. Henson
Edward D. Pelham
Anthony Settlers
Yusef "Yukie" Belton
William Edward Howard
Warren Jackson
An unidentified man
Adolph Martino
Hector Colon
Bruce Lee Parks
Al Johnson
David Kevin Lee
Shonie Clatterbuck
Gregory Jones
David Julien
Donald Johnson
Marx V. Brown

Alonzo D. Allen
David A. Stamper, Jr.
Stephan P. Smith
Ernest E. Young
Martin Freeman
Neil Abbie Thompson
Michael Graham
Gary Wayne Pfleger
Donnell P. Winley
Wayne Huff
Darren Alston
Dwight D. George

# Afterword

## EMPOWERING BLACK CHILDREN: A PRACTICAL HOW-TO GUIDE

### Preparing Our Children for a Complex World

In a world where the echoes of systemic racism reverberate in the subtle and overt dimensions of daily life, the task of raising children can often feel like navigating a relentless storm. As parents, particularly Black parents, our role extends beyond nurturing, providing, and loving. Our hands, which cradle tomorrow's promise, must also forge a shield. This shield is made from resilience, wisdom, and a profound understanding of self. It is a shield that will help our children stride forward amidst the complexities of our society.

The role we play is not an easy one. However, there is a power within us, a formidable strength born of love, resolve, and the collective wisdom of generations that have come before us. We are tasked with arming our children, not with fear, but with knowledge and understanding. We need to prepare them for a world where they might be judged by the color of their skin, but teach them to rise above it and assert their worth and humanity.

This is a journey of empowerment, where each step we take will help them find their footing better. It is a path where the milestones are made of candid conversations, the signposts are crafted from the rich narratives of Black history and culture, and the direction is set by the shining examples of resilience in the face of adversity.

In the following pages, we will explore these practical steps that we, as Black parents, can take to arm our children with the most potent advice and guidance. This is not merely a how-to guide; it is a beacon illuminating our path forward. By walking this path together, we will ensure our children are equipped with the tools to navigate and thrive in a society that is yet to fully overcome the shadow of institutionalized racism.

This is our task, our responsibility, and our greatest act of love. The journey starts now. Let's take this first step together, knowing that with each stride, we are paving the way for a brighter, more equitable future for our children.

# Encourage Open Conversation

As parents, one of our key roles is to serve as the beacon guiding our children through the often murky waters of society. This guiding light is best maintained by fostering an environment where open and honest conversation can flourish. Particularly when it comes to race and systemic racism, providing our children with a safe space to express their feelings, experiences, and concerns is paramount.

The world our children inhabit will inevitably expose them to instances of prejudice and racial bias. These experiences can spark various emotions, from anger to confusion, hurt, and frustration. As guardians of their welfare, we need to validate these emotions. Our children must know that feeling and expressing these emotions is perfectly okay, even necessary.

In this haven we create for them, their fears are not dismissed, their confusion isn't silenced, and their anger isn't quelled. Instead, these feelings are acknowledged, discussed, and worked through together. This forms the crux of our approach to discussing race and racism: an open dialogue that does not shy away from the uncomfortable but tackles it with honesty and understanding.

Our role here is not merely to be the listeners; we are also the first line of defense for our children, reassuring them, providing perspective, and equipping them with the emotional tools to navigate their experiences.

In these open conversations, we arm them with the knowledge that, despite the difficulties they face, they are not alone. They have a strong, supportive base at home, a place where their experiences are understood, their feelings are respected, and their voices are heard.

Here are some practical steps to promote open dialogue:

- **Create a Safe Space:** The starting point of nurturing communication is creating a home environment that serves as a sanctuary. In this space, your children can freely express their innermost thoughts, fears, and emotions without the fear of judgment or dismissal. Your home should be a fortress of comfort where they can share their unique experiences and perspectives. Not only should they feel physically safe, but they should also feel emotionally secure. Their voices should echo with certainty and confidence in your home, knowing they will be heard and understood.

- **Start Conversations:** As a caregiver, it is essential not to remain passive, waiting for your child to broach the subjects of race and racism. Instead, proactively create opportunities to discuss these matters, integrating them as a regular, integral part of your family's dialogue. This could be as simple as discussing relevant current events, exploring themes of race in the books you read together, or discussing their experiences at school. Be the catalyst that sparks these conversations, making them a norm rather than an exception.

- **Be Honest and Open:** While engaging in these conversations, an essential aspect is striking a balance between honesty and affirmation. Be candid about the harsh realities of racism and how it could impact them. However, ensure that this openness is balanced by constant affirmations of their intrinsic value and worth. This sends a powerful message—their worth is inherent and unalterable, regardless of the biases they may encounter. This balance is key to fostering their self-esteem while arming them with necessary knowledge.

- **Listen Actively:** Listening is a skill that's as crucial, if not more, than speaking. When your child communicates their feelings or experiences, ensure that you are not just hearing their words but genuinely listening to their messages. Show genuine interest in their thoughts and emotions. Maintain eye contact, nod in agreement, provide comforting words, and respond appropriately. Active listening helps your child feel seen, heard, and validated, fostering more profound connections.

- **Validate Their Feelings:** Validation is pivotal when it comes to your child's feelings, especially those stemming from difficult experiences. If they express anger, confusion, or sadness about an encounter or event, affirm these emotions as normal and understandable responses. Empathize with them and reassure them that feeling these emotions is okay. This validation helps them to process their feelings healthily and teaches them that their emotions are valuable.

- **Ask Open-Ended Questions:** A practical way to deepen conversations about race and racism is by asking open-ended questions. These questions allow your child to express their thoughts fully and show them that you value their perspectives. Instead of simple "yes" or "no" questions, ask them "how," "why," and "what" questions that encourage more thoughtful responses and stimulate meaningful dialogue.

- **Encourage Expression in Different Forms:** Understand that verbal communication may not always be the preferred or most comfortable way for your children to express their feelings. They might find it easier to express themselves through creative outlets like writing, drawing, music, or play. Encourage this variety of expression, fostering a multi-faceted approach to communication that resonates with your child's unique preferences and talents.

- **Be Patient:** Encouraging open and honest communication is a process that demands patience. Children may struggle to articulate their experiences and emotions, particularly when dealing with complex issues like race and racism. Be patient with them, giving them the time and space they need to find the right words, express their feelings, and share their experiences. Remember that this is a learning journey for them, one where they should feel supported and understood.

- **Lead by Example:** As a role model, your actions and behaviors leave a lasting impact on your child. By communicating openly, honestly, and respectfully, you set a precedent for your child to emulate. This demonstration of effective communication encourages them to adopt similar practices, fostering a family culture of open dialogue and mutual respect.

- **Keep the Conversation Going:** Lastly, it's essential to ensure these dialogues about race and racism are not one-off conversations. They should be ongoing and evolve with your child's growing experiences and understanding. Regularly check in with your children, allowing them to share their experiences, thoughts, and feelings. Making these conversations a consistent part of your relationship with your child empowers them to navigate their experiences with race and racism confidently and thoughtfully.

Let's remind ourselves regularly that these conversations are not one-time discussions; they are ongoing dialogues. We should revisit these conversations, evolving them in line with our children's experiences and growth. By encouraging open conversation, we instill in our children the confidence to face the world, knowing they can always find solace, strength, and understanding in our shared dialogue.

# Educate Them on Black History and Culture

Nurturing your child's understanding of their cultural heritage and history is critical to arming them with self-esteem and a sense of belonging. In a society where the dominant narratives often marginalize or obscure the experiences and contributions of Black people, intentional education about Black history and culture can serve as an empowering antidote.

Begin by infusing their daily life with the richness of Black culture. This could be through music, art, food, and languages associated with their ancestry. Encourage their curiosity and cultivate a sense of pride and appreciation for the variety and depth of Black culture. This step can help your child see themselves as part of a vibrant, diverse, and influential community.

Next, create opportunities for them to learn about the legacy and achievements of Black individuals who have contributed significantly to society. There's much to explore, from historical figures such as Martin Luther King Jr., Rosa Parks, and Malcolm X to contemporary icons such as Barack Obama, Mae Jemison, and Chimamanda Ngozi Adichie.

There are several effective methods to impart this knowledge:

- **Children's Books:** An excellent entry point to the vast and rich history of Black culture and accomplishment is through children's books. Carefully selected literature can effortlessly weave stories of Black heroes, achievements, and cultural narratives into the minds of young readers. Books like *Little Leaders: Bold Women in Black History* by Vashti Harrison and *I Am Rosa Parks* by Brad Meltzer serve as excellent resources. These narratives, accessible and engaging, introduce Black history and culture in a relatable and digestible manner. Incorporating these books into their reading routine effectively plants the seeds of cultural pride and identity in your children.

- **Educational Movies and Documentaries:** Movies and documentaries have the unique power to bring history to life, offering visual storytelling that can captivate young minds. Films like *Hidden Figures* and *Harriet* depict Black individuals' struggles, triumphs, and resilience throughout history. These movies not only educate but also stimulate interest and promote discussion on the complexities and realities of Black history. Introducing your children to these films provides a dynamic and compelling way to engage with history and culture.

- **Online Resources:** In the digital age, educational websites and online tools offer a treasure trove of resources for interactive learning. Websites like BlackPast, PBS's African American World, and National Geographic's Black History provide extensive information, interactive content, and engaging activities. These platforms can help your children explore Black history and culture in a fun, engaging, and modern way, transforming learning into a delightful and enriching experience.

- **Museums and Cultural Events:** If circumstances permit, visiting museums and cultural events dedicated to Black history and culture can provide a rich, immersive, and tangible learning experience. These outings offer a unique opportunity to interact with history and culture more personally. Museums often house artifacts, exhibitions, and narratives that breathe life into history, while cultural events celebrate traditions and heritage in a lively and exciting manner. These experiences can significantly deepen your children's understanding and appreciation of their roots and culture.

- **Family History:** Lastly, exploring your family history can be a source of pride, strength, and inspiration for your children. Sharing stories of your ancestors and relatives who have overcome adversities, made significant contributions to their communities, or simply lived with courage and resilience can instill a sense of identity and belonging. Family history provides a personal and emotional connection to the broader narrative of Black history and culture. As such, it's a potent tool to teach your children about their roots, strength, and potential.

Educating your children about Black history and culture equips them with a sense of pride in their identity and an understanding of their roots. This knowledge can be a source of strength and inspiration, empowering them to navigate the world confidently and self-assuredly. They will not only know where they come from, but also recognize the immense potential and promise within them as part of the Black community.

# Teach Them About Racism and Bias

Living in a world steeped in systemic racism requires children of color to navigate a minefield of biases and prejudices. In such a challenging environment, as a parent, one of your crucial responsibilities is to educate your children about racism and bias, providing them with the necessary context to make sense of the realities they will encounter.

Though it may seem daunting, starting these conversations at an early age is essential, preparing them to understand, question, and challenge the racial dynamics they will inevitably face. This process should be approached thoughtfully, using age-appropriate language and resources that can help them grasp the complexities of racism and its effects.

Here are some strategies that can be employed to guide your children through this learning journey:

- **Define Racism and Bias:** Start the education process by explaining the fundamental concepts of racism and bias in age-appropriate language. For younger children, this might mean illustrating racism as a form of unfair treatment based on differences in skin color or ethnic background. As your children mature, gradually delve into more complex aspects such as systemic racism, unconscious bias, discrimination, and stereotypes. Breaking down these terms and concepts in understandable language will equip your children with a clearer understanding of the world and the social issues that may impact them.

- **Discuss the Impact of Racism:** As your children learn about the realities of racism, it's crucial to discuss its impacts on individuals and societies. Use age-appropriate examples, and facilitate a safe space for them to imagine how they might feel in similar situations. This exercise will foster empathy, allowing them to comprehend the injustices caused by racism on a deeper level. It's important to discuss not only the overt forms of racism but also the subtle, insidious ways it manifests, such as microaggressions or implicit biases.

- **Identify Examples of Racism and Bias:** To further their understanding, use examples from various sources like books, movies, or real-life scenarios to illustrate instances of racism and bias. This could range from identifying racist stereotypes portrayed in media to discussing news events that showcase racial discrimination. By contextualizing racism within relatable scenarios, you enable your children to recognize and understand these issues when they see them.

- **Acknowledge the Prevalence of Racism:** Ensure your children understand that racism is not just a historical issue—it continues to exist today. Although strides have been made toward racial equality, it's essential to convey that there's still considerable work to be done. By acknowledging the continued prevalence of racism, you're setting the stage for them to become informed and empathetic individuals capable of contributing to the fight against racial injustice.

- **Emphasize the Unfairness:** Reiterate that racism is fundamentally unfair and unjust. Be clear that the person subjected to discrimination is not at fault—they should never feel at fault for their skin color or ethnic background. By emphasizing the inherent injustice of racism, you are instilling in your children a sense of fairness and a moral compass to challenge inequity when they encounter it.

- **Encourage Critical Thinking:** Cultivate critical thinking skills in your children. Encourage them to question the information they encounter daily—how diverse are the characters in their favorite books or shows? How are people of different races portrayed in the media they consume? These questions prompt a deeper examination of their surroundings and promote awareness of bias, stereotypes, and unequal representation.

- **Promote Action:** Lastly, empower your children to actively oppose racism when they encounter it. This could take several forms: defending a friend subjected to racial bullying, challenging unfair stereotypes they come across, or joining you in peaceful protests or community meetings advocating for racial justice. By equipping them with knowledge and agency, you raise future champions in the fight against racial discrimination.

By proactively educating your children about racism and bias, you equip them to recognize, comprehend, and confront the racial dynamics they will undoubtedly face. With this knowledge, they can confidently navigate the world, stand against injustice, and contribute to creating a fairer and more equitable society. Remember, this learning journey is ongoing, and it is important to continually revisit and expand on these discussions as your child grows and matures.

# Foster Self-Esteem and Self-Worth

One of the most transformative tools you can equip your children with as they traverse the complexities of a racially biased society is a solid foundation of self-esteem and self-worth. This section focuses on fostering an unbeatable sense of self in your child, empowering them to combat the negativity they may encounter due to societal prejudices and stereotypes.

Self-esteem, an individual's subjective evaluation of their worth, shapes how they view themselves and interact with the world. As your child grows in an environment often marred by systemic racism, this self-esteem becomes armor. This protective layer repels negativity and anchors their identity firmly amidst societal biases.

Here are some strategies you can adopt to cultivate self-esteem and self-worth in your children:

- **Promote Self-Love:** It's crucial to emphasize the importance of self-love and self-acceptance in your child's journey of understanding and navigating racism. Teach your children to fully embrace their identities, regardless of external judgments or stereotypes they may encounter. Encourage them to recognize their uniqueness and celebrate their individuality. They should understand that they are worthy of respect, love, and kindness just as they are, not because of or despite their racial background.

- **Reiterate Their Inherent Value:** Regularly affirm your child's worth as part of building their self-esteem. Take time to acknowledge their strengths, talents, and positive attributes. Celebrate their achievements, no matter how small, and reassure them during their struggles. Impress upon them that others' perceptions or societal prejudices don't determine their value; it is inherent and unchanging. This repeated affirmation helps to build their resilience and buffers against any negative messaging they may receive from the world around them.

- **Encourage Positive Affirmations:** Introduce your child to the empowering practice of positive affirmations. Teach them to use encouraging language towards themselves, affirming their capabilities, worth, and potential. Whether it's starting the day with a statement like "I am brave and capable," or responding to a challenge with "I can learn and grow from this," such affirmations can significantly enhance their self-confidence, resilience, and overall positive outlook.

- **Celebrate Their Racial and Cultural Heritage:** Encourage great pride in your child's racial and cultural heritage. Engage them in learning about their culture's history, achievements, and strengths. Familiarize them with notable figures and historical milestones, and celebrate traditional practices, arts, music, and foods. This knowledge can bolster their sense of identity, enhance their self-worth, and shield them against any racial bias or negative stereotypes they may encounter.

- **Challenge Racial Stereotypes:** Equip your children with the knowledge and critical thinking skills to question and challenge racial stereotypes. Reinforce the understanding that these stereotypes are often misguided and biased generalizations that aim to categorize individuals unfairly. Empower them to push back against such stereotypes, helping them understand that these misrepresentations do not define them or limit their potential.

- **Promote Personal Growth:** Encourage your children to prioritize personal growth over perfection. This means cultivating a growth mindset in them, one that views challenges as opportunities for learning and improvement, and values effort and progress over immediate success. This perspective fosters resilience and helps to enhance their self-esteem, further strengthening their ability to navigate a world where they may face racial biases.

- **Model Self-Worth and Confidence:** Remember, children often learn more from what they see than what they're told. Therefore, modeling self-confidence, self-respect, and a healthy sense of self-worth gives your child a strong example to emulate. Show them how to navigate the world with dignity and strength. Show them that standing up for oneself and one's community is not just possible, but essential. By doing so, you're not just instructing your child about self-worth and confidence; you're embodying these traits for them to see, learn, and imitate.

Fostering self-esteem is a continuous process that evolves as your child grows. The journey will be fraught with challenges, particularly in a society where racial bias persists. However, by consistently nurturing their self-worth and providing an environment that celebrates their uniqueness and strengths, you arm your children with a powerful armor that shields them from societal prejudices.

## Encourage Resilience and Perseverance

In a society where institutionalized racism remains an unsettling reality, cultivating resilience and perseverance in our children is not merely necessary—it's essential. This chapter centers on reinforcing these qualities in your children, empowering them to assert their rights, confront adversities head-on, and persist steadfastly, even when faced with daunting odds.

Resilience—the capacity to recover quickly from difficulties—is a psychological strength that helps individuals cope with hardships and bounce back from setbacks. On the other hand, perseverance is about the relentless pursuit of goals despite obstacles and challenges. In a racially biased environment, these attributes serve as both a shield and a spear, helping Black children withstand adversity and propel forward, forging a path for themselves amidst societal challenges.

Here are some strategies that can aid in building resilience and instilling the spirit of perseverance in your children:

- **Share Stories of Triumph Against All Odds:** Narrating the inspirational stories of Black individuals who, despite facing significant challenges and obstacles, managed to achieve remarkable feats and contribute meaningfully to society can significantly impact your child's understanding of their potential. These stories, which encapsulate the essence of resilience and perseverance, not only serve as sources of inspiration but also offer tangible, real-life examples of individuals who didn't allow societal prejudices or biases to thwart their ambitions. Whether it's recounting Rosa Parks's life, Muhammad Ali's audacity, or Mae Jemison's genius, these narratives can empower your child and foster a sense of determination and courage in them.

- **Teach Them to Stand Up for Their Rights:** As part of your child's preparation to navigate a world where racial bias exists, educating them about their rights is essential. Teach them to recognize instances of prejudice and discrimination and equip them with the skills to assertively yet respectfully stand up for their rights when they perceive them to be violated. This could be through role-playing different scenarios or discussing real-life instances where individuals stood up against discrimination. This consciousness and readiness to advocate for oneself are critical life skills for all children.

- **Reinforce the Power of Persistence:** A critical life lesson to impart to your child is the importance of determination and resilience. Convey the belief that they can overcome challenges and achieve their goals if they stay persistent and committed to their endeavors, even in the face of failure or setbacks. Share personal and historical stories of individuals who succeeded, not because they never failed, but because they never quit. This instills in them the understanding that perseverance is often the bridge between failure and success.

- **Promote Problem-Solving Skills:** Resilience is significantly enhanced when children approach problems with a solution-focused mindset. Encourage them to view challenges not as insurmountable obstacles but as opportunities for growth and learning. This could involve brainstorming solutions, weighing pros and cons, and taking calculated risks. This skill fosters resilience, allowing them to navigate hurdles effectively and feel a sense of control, even in challenging situations.

- **Cultivate Emotional Intelligence:** An essential aspect of fostering resilience is helping children develop emotional intelligence—the ability to positively understand, use, and manage their own emotions. This involves recognizing and validating their feelings, teaching them to express their emotions appropriately, and equipping them with strategies to manage stress and bounce back from adversity. Emotional intelligence helps them cope with stress and enhances their ability to navigate social complexities, thus fostering resilience.

- **Provide a Safe and Supportive Environment:** A crucial part of nurturing resilient children is ensuring your home is a safe space where they feel loved, heard, and understood. They should feel free to express their thoughts and emotions without fear of judgment. Creating a supportive environment allows them to explore their strengths and weaknesses, fail, learn, and grow, all of which are critical to building resilience.

- **Instill Confidence in Their Abilities:** Another essential element of building resilience is fostering a sense of self-efficacy—confidence in their abilities to handle challenges and effect change. This involves acknowledging their efforts, praising their perseverance, and encouraging them to take on progressively more challenging tasks. This belief in their capabilities motivates them to tackle challenges head-on and fuels their spirit of determination and overall resilience.

Fostering resilience and perseverance in your children is not a one-time task but an ongoing process. It's about creating an environment that nurtures these qualities, providing them with the tools to manage stress and adversity and reinforcing the belief that they can overcome obstacles. This cultivation of resilience and perseverance will empower your children to navigate the complexities of institutionalized racism with strength and courage, carving their path toward success.

# Equip Them with Social Skills

To face the prevailing issue of institutionalized racism, Black children must be equipped with robust social skills. This chapter delves into how you can aid in developing effective communication abilities in your children, teaching them to express their emotions constructively and stand up for themselves respectfully yet assertively.

As a critical component of emotional intelligence, social skills are crucial to fostering healthy interpersonal relationships and navigating various social situations. Mastering these abilities can enable your children to voice their thoughts and feelings clearly, assert their rights appropriately, and interact confidently with the world around them.

Below are some of the strategies to cultivate proficient social skills in your children:

- **Foster Emotional Literacy:** Identifying and understanding emotions is a fundamental part of emotional literacy. Providing tools to your children to help them understand the spectrum of emotions they experience—from joy, excitement, and love, to anger, sadness, and fear—enables them to express their feelings accurately and constructively. You can support your children in this journey by normalizing conversations about feelings, using emotion-labeled vocabulary in daily discussions, and validating their emotions as normal and essential. Emotional literacy bolsters self-awareness and is a critical component of effective and empathetic communication.

- **Practice Active Listening:** Active listening goes beyond simply hearing spoken words. It involves understanding the message, empathizing with the speaker, and responding to communicate this understanding and empathy. This is a vital skill that helps in building stronger and healthier relationships. Encourage your children to practice active listening by maintaining eye contact, not interrupting the speaker, providing feedback through nods or words of understanding, and summarizing or asking questions to ensure clarity. Role-playing scenarios can be valuable to demonstrate and practice active listening skills.

- **Teach Assertive Communication:** Empower your children with the skills to express their thoughts, feelings, and needs respectfully yet confidently. This involves teaching them the difference between passive, aggressive, and assertive communication styles. Assertive communication entails expressing oneself openly and honestly without infringing on the rights of others. You can provide guidance on maintaining their calm and dignity in various situations and using "I" statements that express their feelings and needs without blaming or criticizing others—this respectful approach to self-expression aids in fostering mutual respect and understanding.

- **Promote Respectful Disagreement:** Disagreements and conflicts are an inevitable part of life. It's essential to equip your children with strategies to handle disagreements in a respectful and productive manner. This involves focusing on the issue rather than resorting to personal attacks, listening to the other person's perspective, finding common ground, and seeking win-win solutions. Regularly practicing conflict resolution strategies can help children constructively navigate their disagreements and differences.

- **Develop Empathy:** Cultivating empathy is key to enriching interpersonal relationships and developing compassionate responses to injustice or bias. By helping your children understand and share the feelings of others, they learn to connect on a deeper level and to consider perspectives different from their own. This can be achieved through activities like reading diverse stories, role-playing different scenarios, and discussing how they might feel in similar situations.

- **Educate on Rights and Personal Boundaries:** Children must understand their rights and the significance of respecting others' rights and personal boundaries. This involves discussing personal space, consent, and the right to express their feelings and needs. This awareness helps them to respect others' boundaries and to recognize when their boundaries are being violated, which are vital aspects of respectful and effective communication. You can reinforce these concepts through real-life examples, role-playing, and ongoing dialogue.

By honing these social skills, you're preparing your children to interact positively with their peers and adults and equipping them with the tools to assertively navigate a society where they may encounter racial bias. Effective communication empowers them to voice their concerns, assert their rights, and constructively advocate for themselves.

# Provide Tools for Coping with Stress

While raising Black children in a society marked by institutionalized racism, it is vital not to overlook the impact such an environment can have on their mental health. Stress, anxiety, and uncertainty can manifest in various ways in their lives. In this crucial section, we explore how you can equip your children with various techniques to manage stress, bolstering their mental resilience and well-being.

Understanding and addressing mental health is integral to preparing your children for the challenges they may face. By arming them with various coping mechanisms, you are providing them with a line of defense against the adverse psychological effects that could stem from racial prejudice and discrimination.

Here are some ways to help your children effectively manage stress and prioritize their mental health:

- **Promote Mindfulness:** Mindfulness is being fully present in the moment and accepting it without judgment. It's a powerful tool that can help your children manage their thoughts and emotions, thereby reducing stress and promoting a sense of calm. You can start by explaining the basic concept of mindfulness and introducing simple exercises, such as mindful eating, mindful walking, or focusing on the sensations of breathing. There are also numerous mindfulness apps and resources specifically designed for children that you can leverage. Practicing mindfulness can enhance their focus, awareness, and emotional regulation skills.

- **Advocate for Meditation:** Meditation is a time-tested technique known for its calming effects and mental health benefits. It can help children to center their minds, combat anxiety, and cultivate inner peace. Start with simple meditation techniques like focusing on breath, counting breaths, or visualizing peaceful scenes. Even a few minutes of daily meditation can significantly affect their stress levels. As they grow older, they can explore more advanced meditation techniques. Remember, it's not about achieving a perfectly still mind but gently returning focus when it wanders.

- **Encourage Physical Activity:** Physical activity is vital in promoting mental well-being. It can help reduce anxiety, improve mood, and boost energy levels. Encourage your children to engage in physical activities that they enjoy. This could be anything from dancing, playing a sport, biking, swimming, or simply taking a walk in the park. Physical activity stimulates the production of endorphins—known as feel-good hormones—and helps break the cycle of negative thoughts that often accompany stress.

- **Introduce Stress Management Techniques:** There are several techniques available that can help your children manage stress effectively. This includes methods like progressive muscle relaxation—an exercise where they tense and then relax each muscle group, deep breathing exercises, which can lower heart rate and promote relaxation, and guided imagery, where they visualize a peaceful place or situation to help them relax. Demonstrate these techniques to your children and encourage them to use them whenever they feel overwhelmed. Regular practice can help these techniques become a natural part of their stress management toolkit.

- **Foster a Positive Mindset:** Maintaining a positive mindset is crucial in stress management. Encourage your children to practice gratitude by recognizing and appreciating the good in their lives. This could involve keeping a gratitude journal or sharing things they're thankful for during mealtime or before bed. Encourage them to focus on their strengths and successes rather than dwelling on mistakes or challenges. Inspire them to maintain a hopeful perspective, even during tough times. Cultivating optimism can help them handle stress more effectively and build resilience.

- **Emphasize the Importance of Self-Care:** Self-care involves engaging in activities that nurture one's emotional, physical, and mental well-being. Teach your children the importance of taking time out for themselves, whether it's reading a favorite book, listening to calming music, drawing, playing with a pet, or spending time in nature. Explain that self-care isn't selfish—it's a necessary practice that can help restore energy, boost mood, and alleviate stress. Building a self-care routine can significantly contribute to overall well-being.

- **Encourage Open Communication About Feelings:** Create a supportive environment where your children feel comfortable expressing their feelings. Encourage them to share their worries, fears, and stresses with you or a trusted adult. Normalize conversations about emotions and validate their feelings, letting them know it's okay to feel what they're feeling. Open communication can provide emotional relief and help them feel understood and supported.

- **Connect with Mental Health Professionals:** If you notice signs of chronic stress, anxiety, or other mental health issues in your children, don't hesitate to seek professional help. Mental health professionals like psychologists and therapists can provide additional support, guidance, and intervention strategies. Early intervention can make a significant difference in managing and overcoming mental health challenges.

By providing your children with these tools, you are helping them build a sturdy foundation of resilience and mental health. These tools not only equip them to cope with the stressors arising from institutionalized racism but also prepare them to manage life's many challenges in general. Mental health is not a destination but a journey. These skills will continue to serve them as they navigate life, fostering resilience, confidence, and overall well-being.

# Build a Strong Support Network

Raising children in a society where they must constantly navigate the complexities of institutionalized racism is a daunting task. One of the most invaluable resources you can provide for your children is a robust support network—a cadre of trusted individuals who can provide guidance, empathy, and understanding. This network serves as an emotional cushion, a haven, and a source of reassurance, granting your children the confidence to confront challenges and adversities head-on.

The significance of a strong support network cannot be understated. It plays a pivotal role in shaping Black children's worldviews, perspectives, and coping mechanisms and, in many cases, serves as a line of defense against the psychological impacts of racism. This network comprises family members, mentors, teachers, peers, and other influential figures who empathize with their experiences and are committed to their growth and well-being.

Here's how you can help your children build a robust support network:

- **Family as the First Line of Support:** As parents and primary caregivers, you are your children's primary source of support. This means that maintaining regular check-ins and initiating open discussions about their experiences, feelings, and concerns is crucial. Through these conversations, you can foster a nurturing and understanding home environment where your children feel safe expressing their thoughts and emotions. Make it abundantly clear that your home is a space of unconditional love and acceptance, where they can always turn to you for guidance, reassurance, or just a listening ear. Create an atmosphere of trust where your children understand their thoughts and feelings are valued and respected.

- **Mentorship as Guiding Lights:** Mentors can serve as powerful guiding forces in a child's life, providing valuable insights and guidance based on their experiences navigating the challenges of racism. These mentors could be community leaders, family friends, or accomplished individuals within their fields who can serve as positive role models. Through mentorship, your children can learn from others' lived experiences, gain diverse perspectives, and acquire practical advice on confronting and overcoming racial biases and prejudices. Encourage your children to interact regularly with their mentors, engage in meaningful conversations, and learn from their wisdom and experiences.

- **Teachers as Advocates:** Teachers and school administrators play a significant role in shaping a child's educational journey. Collaborate with educators committed to creating inclusive, equitable, and supportive learning environments. Teachers who recognize and value Black students' diverse experiences and perspectives can make a significant difference in their academic experience and personal development. Attend parent-teacher meetings, stay updated with your child's school activities, and encourage educators to ensure fair treatment and equal opportunities for all students.

- **Peers as Comrades:** Encourage your children to build relationships with peers who share similar experiences. These relationships can offer understanding, camaraderie, and the comfort of shared experiences. Peers can provide emotional support, share coping mechanisms, and contribute to a sense of belonging. Encourage your children to be open to making friends from different backgrounds, promoting a diverse and inclusive peer group.

- **Community Organizations as Extensions of Support:** Numerous community organizations and social groups focus on empowering Black youth. These organizations often offer resources, programs, mentorship opportunities, and support networks that can further bolster your child's resilience and personal growth. They can also provide platforms for your child to engage with and contribute to their community, fostering a sense of purpose and empowerment. Encourage your children to participate in activities organized by these entities, and take advantage of the resources they offer.

- **Professional Services as Needed:** If you observe that your child is grappling with excessive stress, anxiety, or other mental health issues, do not hesitate to seek professional help. Counselors, therapists, and other mental health professionals can provide specialized guidance and therapeutic strategies to help manage stress and anxiety, particularly those stemming from experiences with racism. These professionals can equip your child with the tools and techniques to manage their emotions, build resilience, and improve their overall mental well-being. Remember, seeking help is not a sign of weakness but a proactive step toward ensuring your child's mental health and well-being.

By fostering a robust support network, you are gifting your children a safety net of individuals who stand ready to catch them when they stumble, celebrate their achievements, and guide them through the intricacies of life. The people in this network serve as confidants, cheerleaders, guides, and advocates, providing emotional assistance and a sense of belonging. The presence of a support network instills in them the courage to face adversity, reinforcing their resolve to overcome the challenges posed by institutionalized racism and empowering them to flourish amidst adversity.

# Develop Critical Thinking Skills

Nurturing a child's mind to comprehend, analyze, and question the world around them is essential to modern parenting. This is particularly true for Black parents raising their children in societies plagued with institutionalized racism. Critical thinking, an indispensable life skill, empowers your children to discern, dissect, and deconstruct biases, stereotypes, and instances of unfair treatment they may encounter.

- *What Every Black Parent Needs to Know About Saving Our Sons* identifies the development of critical thinking skills as a crucial tactic in arming Black children against the harsh realities of racial prejudice. Encouraging critical thinking allows them to challenge unjust constructs and systems effectively and play an active role in advocating for their rights.

Here's how you can foster critical thinking in your children:

- **Encourage Curiosity and Inquisitiveness:** Curiosity and inquisitiveness are the cornerstones of critical thinking and intellectual growth. To foster this mindset, encourage your children to ask questions, to be curious about the world around them, and always to seek out knowledge. Foster a learning environment where questions are encouraged and every answer is seen as a stepping stone to more learning. This could involve asking them open-ended questions, presenting them with intriguing scenarios, or engaging in conversations about their interests. Remember, curiosity leads to exploration, which in turn leads to learning and growth.

- **Teach Them to Analyze:** Equip your children with the ability to break down complex information, situations, and arguments into smaller, manageable parts for better understanding. Encourage them to dissect and examine each part to better comprehend the whole. Teach them to assess situations from multiple perspectives, consider different variables, and understand cause-and-effect relationships. You could do this through puzzles, thought experiments, or by encouraging them to break down their day's events into smaller components and examine how they link together.

- **Promote Independent Thought:** An essential aspect of critical thinking is the capacity for independent thought. Foster an environment at home where independent thinking is accepted, valued, and respected. Encourage your children to form their own opinions, based on their analysis and understanding, rather than merely accepting information at face value. This encourages a sense of autonomy and personal responsibility and helps them to develop the confidence to stand by their ideas and beliefs.

- **Expose Them to Diverse Viewpoints:** Broadening your children's horizons and exposing them to a wide array of ideas, cultures, philosophies, and perspectives can significantly enhance their critical thinking abilities. This can involve reading books from various genres and cultures, watching documentaries about different societies, or engaging in conversations about global issues. Understanding and appreciating different perspectives helps foster empathy, increase cultural competency, and enrich intellectual perspectives.

- **Discuss and Debate:** Engage your children in discussions and debates about relevant and age-appropriate issues ranging from daily decisions to broader societal issues. Encourage them to articulate their thoughts, arguments, and counterarguments clearly and coherently. This process sharpens their reasoning and argumentative skills and boosts their confidence in expressing their ideas and defending their viewpoints.

- **Encourage Reflection:** Reflection is a powerful tool for growth. Teach your children the value of introspection and self-evaluation. Encourage them to reflect on their experiences, decisions, and beliefs regularly. They can learn to identify their strengths, acknowledge their areas of improvement, and understand the rationale behind their choices. This aids in refining their thought processes over time and fosters a culture of continuous learning and self-improvement.

- **Model Critical Thinking:** As a parent, you are your children's most influential role model. Exhibit your critical thinking skills in everyday situations and decision-making processes. Whether making a significant life decision or figuring out the day's schedule, involve your children in the process, show them how you break down the problem, consider various perspectives, and make a reasoned decision. This provides a practical and relatable precedent for your children to emulate, giving them a firsthand demonstration of critical thinking in action.

Critical thinking is more than a skill; it's an intellectual armor protecting your children from passively accepting biased narratives and stereotypes. It equips them to identify and challenge racial disparities and unfair treatment, empowering them to advocate for their rights. Through critical thinking, your children learn to navigate the maze of racial prejudice with insight, resilience, and courage. By arming them with this critical skill, you are preparing them for the challenges of the present and equipping them to shape a fairer, more equitable future.

## Advocate for Your Children

In a world that seems inclined to diminish the worth of your children due to the color of their skin, one of your most powerful roles as a parent is that of an advocate. As parents, we are bestowed with the duty to protect our children from harm and challenge the systems and structures that breed such harm. Advocacy isn't merely about shielding; it's about altering the status quo. It's about battling for equity and justice.

The Black child growing up in a society riddled with institutionalized racism may encounter numerous obstacles, not because of their capacity or merits but due to a racially biased system. Here, as guardians and guides, your voice can make a profound difference. Stand up for your children, raise your voice when you perceive injustice, and fight for their rights when necessary.

Taking a stand in such scenarios doesn't only guard your child against unfair treatment; it also serves as a powerful model for your children. When they see you standing up for their rights, they're not just witnessing protection in action; they're learning the vital skills of self-advocacy. You're not merely their shield but also their guide, teaching them to eventually raise their own shields.

As your children mature, they will need to navigate many of these battles independently. Your actions and advocacy lay the foundation for them to stand up for their rights and the rights of others. They learn to identify when they're being treated unfairly, believe in their worth, and demand the respect they deserve.

In advocating for your children, you're teaching them the language of justice and resilience. You're providing them with the tools they need to fight against a system that may try to undermine their worth. The powerful voice of advocacy, whether it echoes in a classroom, a legislative chamber, or a neighborhood, imparts them with the courage to assert themselves and resist inequity.

Most importantly, your advocacy conveys to your children that they are valued and that they matter. It tells them that their rights are worth fighting for and that they should never allow the color of their skin to dictate their worth or their dreams.

Therefore, advocating for your children isn't merely about battling the systemic racism they may face today; it's about equipping them with the resilience, courage, and self-esteem they need to challenge, overcome, and dismantle these oppressive systems in the future.

As you stand as a beacon for your children, remember this—you're not only their protector but their exemplar. You're shaping the advocates of the future, those who will continue to fight for justice, equity, and dignity for all.

## Armoring Our Children for a Resilient Future

As parents, guardians, mentors, and teachers, you are the vanguard in this quest. Your role is paramount in arming these young minds with the right tools—an amalgamation of wisdom, self-esteem, resilience, and practical skills that can serve as an armor that protects, a sword that challenges, and a compass that guides. You stand as the purveyors of knowledge, inculcating in them the understanding of their rich heritage, the awareness of the biases they might face, and the courage to challenge these societal stereotypes.

Empowering your children goes beyond merely providing them with information. It is about teaching them to love themselves, recognize their worth, and refuse to be defined by the prejudices they may encounter. By fostering their self-esteem and highlighting their strengths, you provide an inner compass guiding them toward a healthy sense of self.

Instilling resilience and perseverance in the hearts of your children prepares them to face adversity head-on and to persist even when the tides are against them. Equip them with the tenacity of spirit, exemplified by the countless Black individuals who, against the odds, have carved a path for themselves, inspiring generations to come.

Your role extends to fostering their social skills, teaching them to articulate their feelings, stand up for their rights respectfully, and navigate the complex dynamics of race and identity. It is about supporting them, helping them develop a network of positive influences, and demonstrating advocacy for their rights.

Above all, you are their guiding light in the stormy seas of life, their beacon of hope in times of darkness, and their anchor when the waves of life threaten to pull them under. Your love, guidance, and support form the pillars of their strength, shaping them into the changemakers of tomorrow. Your tireless endeavor prepares them to face the world, rise against its prejudices, and advocate for their rights and the rights of their peers.

In this mission of raising confident, successful, and resilient children, remember that each step you take, each lesson you impart, each discussion you initiate, and each challenge you help them overcome, fortifies their armor and sharpens their sword. For at the end of the day, your children are not just surviving the world, they are learning to change it. They are the promise of a brighter, fairer future, a testament to your resilience, and the legacy of your love.

**M.J. Fievre, author of *Raising Confident Black Kids***

# Resources

Navigating the nuanced challenges of parenthood is an enriching journey, yet it can often feel like you're traversing a path with minimal guidance and numerous obstacles. This is especially true for Black parents who face the additional hurdle of raising children in a society marred by institutionalized racism. This resource guide aims to provide a comprehensive roadmap, offering essential tools, resources, and insights to empower and equip you to guide and nurture your children effectively.

We've crafted this guide, drawing from various mediums and platforms, to ensure you have access to diverse and relevant resources. Each category addresses specific aspects of your journey in raising confident, successful, and resilient Black children.

**Books** provide profound insights and knowledge on various subjects, be it parenting, racism, empowerment, or Black history. These texts have been carefully chosen to broaden your perspective, offering practical advice and food for thought.

**The Online Resources** section provides an array of digital spaces— from educational websites and legal advice platforms to community forums and nonprofit organizations—that you can turn to for information, support, and community.

Dive into the world of **Podcasts and Videos**. Hear powerful stories, learn from experts, and explore complex topics in an engaging and accessible format.

In this digital age, **Apps and Digital Tools** can be incredible aids. This section introduces you to valuable apps that can support education, mental health, community building, and safety.

During times of crisis or immediate need, **Crisis Helplines** can be lifesaving. We provide a list of reliable helplines for various needs, including mental health, legal advice, emergencies, and general support.

The **Workshops and Seminars** section provides opportunities to engage, learn, and grow. Attend these to understand racism better, improve parenting skills, and empower yourself and your community.

The road of parenthood need not be a solitary journey. In our **Support Groups** section, you'll find resources for both local and online communities that provide empathy, understanding, and shared experiences.

Finding the proper mental health support can be daunting. Our **Therapy Options** section aims to make that journey easier, providing resources to find therapists and understand different therapy approaches.

With the **Advocacy and Activism** section, you can join the fight against institutionalized racism. Discover nonprofits, community groups, and educational institutions making a difference.

Finally, the **Research and Studies** section introduces you to academic resources that can deepen your understanding of institutionalized racism, including academic papers, case studies, and the latest research findings.

Each resource is a step towards understanding, guiding, and nurturing your children in a world that might often seem like it's set up against them. Use this guide as a map, a compass, or a flashlight—helping illuminate the path, pointing in the right direction, and making the journey a little less arduous. Remember, every step you take is a step towards raising strong, confident, and empowered sons who will rise above the challenges and thrive.

# Books

## On Parenting

- *The Conscious Parent: Transforming Ourselves, Empowering Our Children* by Dr. Shefali Tsabary is a guide to conscious parenting that emphasizes the spiritual growth of both parent and child.

- *Parenting from the Inside Out: How a Deeper Self-Understanding Can Help You Raise Children Who Thrive* by Daniel J. Siegel and Mary Hartzell explores the extent to which our childhood experiences shape the way we parent.

- *Raising White Kids: Bringing Up Children in a Racially Unjust America* by Jennifer Harvey is a helpful book for understanding and discussing racism with children.

- *Raising Your Spirited Child: A Guide for Parents Whose Child Is More Intense, Sensitive, Perceptive, Persistent, and Energetic* by Mary Sheedy Kurcinka is a guide for parents providing emotional support and proven strategies for handling the most challenging times.

- *The Whole Brained Child: 12 Revolutionary Strategies to Nurture Your Child's Developing Mind* by Daniel J. Siegel and Tina Payne Bryson offers a revolutionary approach to child-rearing with twelve key strategies that foster healthy brain development, leading to calmer, happier children.

## On Racism and Institutionalized Racism

- *Black Power: The Politics of Liberation in America* by Stokely Carmichael (later known as Kwame Ture) and Charles V. Hamilton defines Black Power, presents insights into the roots of racism in the United States, and suggests a means of reforming the traditional political process for the future.

- *The Color of Law: A Forgotten History of How Our Government Segregated America* by Richard Rothstein argues with exacting precision and fascinating insight that segregation in America is the byproduct of explicit government policies at the local, state, and federal levels.

- *The New Jim Crow: Mass Incarceration in the Age of Colorblindness* by Michelle Alexander explores the racial bias in America's criminal justice system.

- *Stamped from the Beginning: The Definitive History of Racist Ideas in America* by Ibram X. Kendi is a comprehensive history of anti-Black, racist ideas in America.

- *White Fragility: Why It's So Hard for White People to Talk About Racism* by Robin DiAngelo is about understanding the dynamics of race and the reactions of white people when discussing racism.

## On Empowerment and Self-Esteem

- *The Art of Happiness: A Handbook for Living* by Dalai Lama is a book that explores the nature of happiness and how to defeat day-to-day anxiety, insecurity, anger, and discouragement through conversations, stories, and meditations.

- *The Gifts of Imperfection: Let Go of Who You Think You're Supposed to Be and Embrace Who You Are* by Brené Brown is a guide to living an authentic, wholehearted life.

- *The Power of Self-Esteem: An Inspiring Look at Our Most Important Psychological Resource* by Nathaniel Branden explores the role and importance of self-esteem.

- *The Six Pillars of Self-Esteem: The Definitive Work on Self-Esteem by the Leading Pioneer in the Field* by Nathaniel Branden introduces six action-based practices for daily living that provide the foundation for self-esteem and explores the central importance of self-esteem in five areas: the workplace, parenting, education, psychotherapy, and the culture at large.

- *We Real Cool: Black Men and Masculinity* by bell hooks is a look at how Black masculinity is often misunderstood, critiqued, and villainized.

- *You Can Heal Your Life* by Louise Hay is a self-help book that offers insight into how limiting thoughts and ideas control and constrict us and provides a powerful key to understanding the roots of our physical diseases and discomforts.

## On Black History

- *Between the World and Me* by Ta-Nehisi Coates is an intimate, personal exploration of America's racial history.

- *The Fire Next Time* by James Baldwin is an influential work on the Black experience and race relations in America.

- *Four Hundred Souls: A Community History of African America, 1619-2019* by Ibram X. Kendi and Keisha N. Blain is a unique one-volume "community" history of African Americans, told by ninety leading Black voices, that considers the four-hundred-year journey of African Americans from 1619 to the present.

- *How the Word Is Passed: A Reckoning with the History of Slavery Across America* by Clint Smith is a narrative nonfiction text that focuses on historical sites and landmarks connected to the transatlantic slave trade, assessing how these sites deal with the topic of slavery.

- *The Warmth of Other Suns: The Epic Story of America's Great Migration* by Isabel Wilkerson is a moving account of the great migration of African Americans from the South to the North during the twentieth century.

# Online Resources

Each of these resources offers tools to supplement your knowledge and understanding. Check them frequently, as new information and resources are continually added.

## Educational Websites

- Coursera (www.coursera.org) offers online courses from top universities around the world.

- Facing History and Ourselves (www.facinghistory.org) provides resources that connect past to present for a deeper understanding of racism and prejudice.

- Khan Academy (www.khanacademy.org) is a free online learning resource offering lessons in various subjects.

- PBS LearningMedia (www.pbslearningmedia.org) offers free, standards-aligned videos, interactives, and lesson plans.

- Raising Race Conscious Children (www.raceconscious.org) is a resource for parents who aim to talk openly about race with their children.

- Teaching Tolerance (www.tolerance.org) is a Southern Poverty Law Center project offering free resources for teachers and parents to help teach children about race and tolerance.

## Community Forums and Blogs

- African American Homeschool Moms (www.africanamericanhomeschoolmoms.com) is a community of African American parents who homeschool their children.

- Black and Married with Kids (www.blackandmarriedwithkids.com) presents a positive image of Black marriage and parenting.

- Black Parents Forum (www.blackparentsforum.info) is a place for parents to exchange ideas and support each other.

- Colorlines (www.colorlines.com) is a daily news site offering award-winning reporting, analysis, and solutions to today's racial justice issues.

- Mocha Moms (www.mochamoms.org) is a support group for mothers of color who have chosen not to work full-time outside of the home to devote more time to their families and communities.

- My Brown Baby (mybrownbaby.com) is a blog for parents committed to raising children with an understanding of their African-American heritage.

## Legal Advice Websites

- American Civil Liberties Union (ACLU, www.aclu.org) offers legal advice and resources, particularly on civil liberties issues.

- FindLaw (www.findlaw.com) offers free legal information plus a directory of legal services.

- LawHelp (www.lawhelp.org) provides legal help for low-income individuals and connects them with local legal aid and public interest law offices.

- The LegalAdvice subreddit (www.reddit.com/r/legaladvice) is a platform where you can ask legal questions and get advice from real lawyers.

- NAACP Legal Defense Fund (www.naacpldf.org) provides legal assistance in civil rights.
- National Lawyers Guild (www.nlg.org) offers legal support for progressive social movements.

## Government Resources

- Child Welfare Information Gateway (www.childwelfare.gov) offers resources on child welfare, child abuse and neglect, and adoption.
- Office for Civil Rights (www2.ed.gov/about/offices/list/ocr/index.html) enforces federal civil rights laws ensuring equal education access.
- Office of Minority Health (minorityhealth.hhs.gov) offers resources on health disparities and social determinants of health.
- US Equal Employment Opportunity Commission (www.eeoc.gov) enforces federal laws that make it illegal to discriminate against a job applicant or an employee.
- USA.gov (www.usa.gov) is the official portal for all government information.

## Organizations and Nonprofits

- Black Lives Matter (blacklivesmatter.com) is an organization dedicated to combating and countering acts of violence and creating space for Black innovation and joy.
- The Brotherhood/Sister Sol (brotherhood-sistersol.org) provides youth with comprehensive, holistic, and long-term support services.
- The Conscious Kid (www.theconsciouskid.org) is an education, research, and policy organization dedicated to reducing bias and promoting positive identity development in youth.
- The mission of the National Association for the Advancement of Colored People (NAACP, www.naacp.org) is to secure the political, educational, social, and economic equality of rights to eliminate race-based discrimination.

- National CARES Mentoring Movement (caresmentoring.org) offers social and academic support to help Black youth succeed in college and beyond.

- National Urban League (nul.org) is a historic civil rights organization dedicated to economic empowerment to elevate living standards in historically underserved urban communities.

# Podcasts and Videos

Podcasts and videos can offer dynamic and engaging ways to explore and understand issues related to parenting, racism, empowerment, and motivation.

## Podcasts on Parenting

- Akilah S. Richards hosts the *Fare of the Free Child* podcast (raisingfreepeople.com) that centers Black people, Indigenous people, and People of Color in liberatory living and learning practices.

- *The Mom Hour* (themomhour.com) is a parenting podcast that offers helpful advice for moms of all backgrounds, with episodes dedicated to navigating discussions about race.

- *The Momference Podcast* (www.themomference.com) is a supportive space for Black moms where experts discuss parenting topics in depth.

- *Momfully You* (www.momfullyyou.com), hosted by Dr. Amber Thornton, is a podcast dedicated to helping Black mothers feel seen, heard, and validated in their parenting journey.

## Podcasts on Racism and Institutionalized Racism

- 1619 (www.nytimes.com/2020/01/23/podcasts/1619-podcast. html) is a *New York Times* podcast that explores the history of slavery and its lasting impact on America.

- Code Switch (www.npr.org/sections/codeswitch) is an NPR podcast exploring race and identity in America.

- "Seeing White" (www.sceneonradio.org/seeing-white/) is a series from the *Scene on Radio* podcast that delves deep into the history and implications of whiteness.

## Podcasts on Empowerment and Motivation

- *Affirmation Pod* (www.affirmationpod.com) offers soothing affirmations infused with mindfulness to help you live in self-love.

- *Momentum* (momentum.libsyn.com) is a motivational podcast that explores stories of personal empowerment and overcoming obstacles.

- *Myleik Teele's Podcast* (www.podomatic.com/podcasts/myleik) offers Myleik's insights on becoming a self-made businesswoman and powerful advice for those looking to improve their professional and personal lives.

- *Oprah's SuperSoul Conversations* (www.oprah.com/app/supersoul-sunday.html) is hosted by Oprah Winfrey and offers conversations about life, purpose, and potential with guests.

- *Redefining Wealth* (www.patricewashington.com/redefining-wealth-podcast) is a podcast hosted by Patrice Washington that emphasizes the importance of wealth in areas of life beyond just finance.

## Educational Videos and Documentaries

- *13th* is a Netflix documentary by Ava DuVernay which explores the intersection of race, justice, and mass incarceration in the United States.

- *The African Americans: Many Rivers to Cross* (www.pbs.org/wnet/african-americans-many-rivers-to-cross) is a PBS series that explores the evolution of the African-American people, as well as the multiplicity of cultural institutions, political strategies, and religious and social perspectives they developed.

- *Eyes on the Prize* (www.pbs.org/wgbh/americanexperience/films/eyesontheprize) is a landmark documentary series covering all the significant events in the civil rights movement from 1954 through 1985.

- *I Am Not Your Negro* is a documentary envisioning the book James Baldwin never finished, a radical narration about race in America.

- Teaching Tolerance (www.learningforjustice.org) is a website that provides free resources to educators who work with children from kindergarten through high school, including a wide range of social justice and anti-bias videos and documentaries.

These podcasts and videos offer different perspectives and insightful conversations that can be beneficial to your journey. They can provide you with the knowledge, strategies, and understanding necessary to navigate parenting in a racially biased society. Remember to be open to different viewpoints and use these resources to facilitate discussions with your kids.

# Apps and Digital Tools

Apps and digital tools offer a convenient and portable way to access information, support, and resources. This list includes educational apps, mental health resources, community networking tools, and safety applications that can assist Black parents in nurturing and protecting their children in a racially biased society.

## Educational Apps

- Khan Academy Kids (www.khanacademy.org) is a free, fun, educational app with thousands of activities and books that will inspire a lifetime of learning and discovery for young children.

- Brainscape (www.brainscape.com) offers comprehensive flashcards on various topics, including history, and even lets you make your own.

- Elevate (www.elevateapp.com) is a brain-training program designed to improve focus, speaking abilities, processing speed, memory, math skills, and more.

- Graspable Math (www.graspablemath.com) allows students to rearrange terms on the screen to solve math equations, helping them learn algebra and pre-calculus.

- PBS Kids Games offers interactive games that promote learning in math, science, and more.

## Mindfulness and Mental Health Apps

- Calm (www.calm.com) offers guided meditations, sleep stories, breathing programs, and relaxing music.

- Headspace (www.headspace.com) provides mindfulness and meditation techniques to manage stress, sleep better, focus more, and stay calm.

- Liberate (www.liberatemeditation.com) is a subscription-based meditation app created by and for the Black community.

- Shine (www.shinetext.com) provides daily motivational messages and a library of self-improvement audio tracks.

## Networking and Community Apps

- Nextdoor (nextdoor.com) is a neighborhood hub for trusted connections and the exchange of helpful information, goods, and services.

- Meetup (www.meetup.com) helps people to find and join groups unified by a common interest, such as politics, books, games, movies, health, pets, careers, or hobbies.

- Official Black Wall Street (www.officialblackwallstreet.com) is the largest platform in the world for finding and supporting Black-owned businesses.

- We Read Too (www.wereadtoo.com) is a directory of hundreds of picture, chapter, middle grade, and young adult books written by authors of color featuring main characters of color.

## Safety and Emergency Apps

- Bark (www.bark.us/learn/home) helps parents keep kids safe online by detecting threats and sending alerts.

- bSafe (www.getbsafe.com) is a personal safety app where users create a "social safety network" of individuals who are alerted in case of an emergency or in situations where the user feels unsafe.

- Life360 (www.life360.com) offers location-based alerts and features for checking in with family members and can help to locate lost or stolen phones.

- MobilePatrol collaborates with public safety and law enforcement agencies nationwide, offering publicly available safety information.

- Noonlight (www.noonlight.com) provides a virtual panic button that sends your location and relevant information to local authorities if you're in danger.

These digital tools can be invaluable resources for educating, empowering, and protecting your children. From educational material to mental health support, and from building connections to ensuring safety, they can make parenting easier. Remember, though, that apps are tools, not substitutes for personal interaction, conversation, and parental guidance.

# Crisis Helplines

Crisis helplines are essential resources that can offer immediate help, advice, and support during times of difficulty or emergency. They can provide much-needed assistance, from mental health support to legal advice and emergency services.

## Mental Health Helplines

- Crisis Text Line: Text HOME to 741741

    - Crisis Text Line serves anyone in any crisis, providing access to free, 24/7 support and information via a medium people already use and trust: text.

- National Suicide Prevention Lifeline: 1-800-273-TALK (1-800-273-8255)

    - This national network of local crisis centers provides free and confidential emotional support to people in suicidal crisis or emotional distress twenty-four hours a day, seven days a week.

- Website: suicidepreventionlifeline.org

• The Steve Fund Crisis Textline: Text STEVE to 741741

- This partnership between the Steve Fund and the Crisis Text Line provides a culturally trained crisis counselor for young people of color.

• The Trevor Project: 1-866-488-7386

- This line offers crisis intervention and suicide prevention services to lesbian, gay, bisexual, transgender, queer & questioning (LGBTQ) young people under twenty-five.

- Website: www.thetrevorproject.org

## Legal Advice Helplines

• American Civil Liberties Union (ACLU): (212) 549-2500

- The ACLU provides legal assistance in cases when it considers civil liberties at risk and is often involved in litigation related to racial discrimination and civil rights issues.

- Website: www.aclu.org

• Lawyers' Committee for Civil Rights Under Law: (202) 662-8600

- They provide legal services to address racial discrimination, focusing on education, voting rights, and equal economic opportunity.

• NAACP Legal Defense Fund: (212) 965-2200

- This legal organization fights for racial justice.

- Website: www.naacpldf.org

• National Bar Association: (202) 842-3900

- This is the nation's oldest and most extensive network of predominantly African-American attorneys and judges.

- Website: www.nationalbar.org

## Emergency Services

- 911—For immediate emergencies and life-threatening situations.
    - This national emergency number (United States) provides immediate access to emergency services (fire, police, and medical assistance).
- American Red Cross—For emergency assistance, training, and disaster relief.
    - Phone: 1-800-RED CROSS (1-800-733-2767)
    - Website: www.redcross.org
- FEMA (Federal Emergency Management Agency) For help during and after disasters.
    - Phone: 1-800-621-FEMA (1-800-621-3362)
    - Website: www.fema.gov

## Support Helplines

- Black Emotional and Mental Health Collective (BEAM)
    - BEAM is a collective of advocates, yoga teachers, artists, therapists, lawyers, religious leaders, teachers, psychologists, and activists committed to Black communities' emotional/mental health and healing.
    - Website: www.beam.community
- Childhelp National Child Abuse Hotline: 1-800-4-A-CHILD (1-800-422-4453)
    - This helpline is for professional crisis counselors who can provide intervention, information, and referrals to emergency, social service, and support resources.
    - Website: www.childhelp.org/hotline
- National Alliance on Mental Illness (NAMI) Helpline: 1-800-950-NAMI (6264)
    - This helpline can provide information, referrals, and support to people with mental health conditions, family members and caregivers, mental health providers, and the public.

- National Domestic Violence Hotline: 1-800-799-SAFE (1-800-799-7233)
    - This helpline is for any victims or survivors who need support.
    - Website: www.thehotline.org
- National Parent Helpline: 1-855-4A PARENT (1-855-427-2736)
    - This helpline provides emotional support from a trained advocate and helps you become an empowered and stronger parent.
    - Website: www.nationalparenthelpline.org

These helplines offer immediate support and guidance during times of crisis. Remember that reaching out for help is not a sign of weakness but of strength. Knowing you're not alone is crucial; these resources can provide a lifeline when you need it most.

# Workshops and Seminars

Workshops and seminars can be powerful ways to learn new skills, gain knowledge, and interact with others who share similar experiences or interests. Here are some resources for workshops and seminars on parenting, anti-racism, empowerment, and understanding legal rights.

## Parenting Workshops

- The Parent Practice offers courses that help parents bring out the best in their children. www.theparentpractice.com
- Parenting for Liberation is a hub where Black parents can find connection, inspiration, and support through workshops, podcasts, and more. parentingforliberation.org
- Parenting Now! provides parenting education and support to families with young children. parentingnow.org
- The Parenting Training Network (PTN) offers extensive parenting workshops covering many topics related to raising children. parentingtrainingnetwork.com

- Triple P (Positive Parenting Program) offers parenting courses online, in person, and via one-on-one consultations. www.triplep-parenting.com

## Anti-Racism Workshops

- The Racial Equity Institute offers workshops designed to help leaders and organizations develop tools to challenge patterns of power and grow equity. www.racialequityinstitute.com

- CrossRoads Anti-Racism Organizing and Training provides powerful anti-racism workshops and institutional organizing strategies. crossroadsantiracism.org

- The People's Institute for Survival and Beyond (PISAB) offers "Undoing Racism" workshops to understand what racism is, where it comes from, how it functions, why it persists, and how it can be undone. www.pisab.org

## Empowerment Seminars

- Black Male Empowerment (BME) offers seminars on personal growth, academic success, and leadership. bmecommunity.org/about-us

- The Empowerment Partnership offers seminars on personal development and self-empowerment. www.empowermentpartnership.com

- Empowerment Seminars provides resources for personal and spiritual growth. www.empowermentseminars.com

## Legal Rights Workshops

- The ACLU (American Civil Liberties Union, www.aclu.org) provides workshops on understanding and exercising civil rights.

- The NAACP (naacp.org/programs) offers several empowerment programs and workshops educating individuals about their legal rights and responsibilities.

- National Lawyers Guild (www.nlg.org) provides legal observers for protests, offers know-your-rights trainings, and engages in litigation to support social movements.

- Street Law, Inc. (www.streetlaw.org) offers programs and resources about law, democracy, and human rights worldwide.

Workshops and seminars provide valuable opportunities to gain knowledge and skills, engage in dialogue, and connect with a community. They can be a powerful tool to help you navigate parenting challenges in a society of institutionalized racism. Whether it's learning new parenting techniques, understanding systemic racism, enhancing personal empowerment, or knowing your legal rights, these workshops and seminars are an invaluable resource.

# Support Groups

Support groups can provide solace, community, and valuable insights. Whether local or online, for parents or youth, these spaces can facilitate sharing experiences, learning from others, and receiving emotional backing. Here are some resources to help you find the right support group.

## Local Support Groups

- American Self-Help Group Clearinghouse (selfhelpgroups.org) is a searchable database of US local support groups.

- Meetup (www.meetup.com) is a platform that allows you to search for local support groups in your area.

- NAMI (National Alliance on Mental Illness, www.nami.org/Home) offers local support groups for individuals with mental health conditions, and their families.

- Psychology Today (www.psychologytoday.com/us/groups) hosts a database of support groups across different areas and issues.

- United Way (www.211.org) can direct you to local resources, including support groups. Dial 211 or visit their website.

## Online Support Groups

- 7 Cups (www.7cups.com) connects you to caring listeners for free emotional support.

- Daily Strength (www.dailystrength.org) is a collection of online support groups across various categories.

- SupportGroups.com (www.supportgroups.com) is a growing online community offering numerous free support groups for individuals facing various challenges.

## Parenting Support Groups

- Circle of Moms (www.circleofmoms.com) is an online community where mothers can connect, share stories, and support each other.

- Mocha Moms (www.mochamoms.org) is a support group for mothers of color.

- Parents Anonymous (parentsanonymous.org) is a mutual support group for parents to enhance their parenting skills and enrich their family life.

- Parents Helping Parents (PHP, www.php.com) provides resources, workshops, and support groups for parents.

## Support Groups for Black Youth

- BEAM (Black Emotional and Mental Health Collective, beam. community): BEAM offers various support resources for Black youth, including a directory of virtual and in-person mental health services.

- Black Youth Project (BYP, blackyouthproject.com) is an online platform that highlights the voices and ideas of Black millennials, including an online community for Black youth.

- Young, Black & Lit (www.youngblackandlit.org) is a community dedicated to increasing access to children's books that center, reflect, and affirm Black children.

Whether online or in-person, support groups offer a safe space to express feelings, share experiences, and find mutual understanding and empathy.

They can also provide practical advice and helpful resources from people in similar situations.

# Therapy Options

Therapy can be critical in managing mental health, providing a safe space to explore thoughts, emotions, and experiences, and developing coping strategies. Here are resources to help you locate local and online therapy providers, understand different therapeutic techniques and approaches, and tips for finding the right therapist for your own or your child's needs.

## Local Therapy Providers

- The American Psychological Association (APA) Psychologist Locator (locator.apa.org) is a tool for finding mental health professionals in your local area.

- National Queer and Trans Therapists of Color Network (NQTTCN, www.nqttcn.com/directory) is a healing justice organization committed to transforming mental health for queer and trans people of color in the US.

- Psychology Today (www.psychologytoday.com/us/therapists) hosts a comprehensive directory of therapists, psychiatrists, therapy groups, and treatment centers near you.

## Online Therapy Providers

- Amwell (www.amwell.com) provides access to board-certified, licensed doctors, dieticians, and psychologists through video chats.

- BetterHelp (www.betterhelp.com) offers private, affordable online counseling with licensed therapists.

- Talkspace (www.talkspace.com) is an online therapy platform providing access to licensed therapists via messaging and video sessions.

## Therapy Techniques and Approaches

- "Understanding Psychotherapy and How It Works" from the American Psychological Association (APA, www.apa.org/topics/psychotherapy/understanding) helps you understand what to expect from psychotherapy and how it works.

- The Mayo Clinic (www.mayoclinic.org/tests-procedures/psychotherapy/about/pac-20384616) provides overviews of different types of psychotherapy.

- PsychCentral (psychcentral.com/types-of-therapy) provides descriptions of various therapy techniques and approaches.

## Tips for Finding a Therapist

- "How to Choose a Psychologist" from the American Psychological Association (APA, www.apa.org/topics/choose-therapist) offers guidance on selecting a psychologist.

- "Finding a Mental Health Professional" from the National Alliance on Mental Illness (NAMI, www.nami.org/Your-Journey/Individuals-with-Mental-Illness/Finding-a-Mental-Health-Professional) provides tips for finding a mental health professional and making the most out of your treatment.

- Psych Central's Therapist Finder (psychcentral.com/find-help) is a tool to find a therapist that suits your needs.

# Advocacy and Activism

Advocacy and activism are powerful tools for initiating positive change and fighting against systemic racism. Below are some resources that can help you get involved, from nonprofit organizations to community activism groups, to tips for effective advocacy and educational institutions dedicated to promoting advocacy.

## Nonprofit Organizations

- The American Civil Liberties Union (ACLU) is an organization that works to defend and preserve individual rights and liberties. www.aclu.org

- Black Lives Matter is an international activist movement that advocates for the rights of Black individuals. blacklivesmatter.com

- The National Association for the Advancement of Colored People (NAACP) is one of the nation's largest and most prominent civil rights organizations. www.naacp.org

- National Urban League is a historic civil rights and urban advocacy organization with ninety affiliates serving three hundred communities. nul.org

## Community Activism Groups

- Color of Change is a progressive nonprofit civil rights advocacy organization in the United States that uses online resources to strengthen the political voice of African Americans. colorofchange.org

- Community Change is a national organization that builds the power of low-income people, especially people of color, to fight for a society where everyone can thrive. communitychange.org

- The Movement for Black Lives (M4BL) is a space for Black organizations nationwide to debate and discuss the current political conditions and develop shared interventions and responses. m4bl.org

## Tips for Advocacy

- "Advocacy and Policy Change," from the Community Tool Box provides guidance on advocating for policies in the public interest. ctb.ku.edu/en/advocacy

- "Advocacy Tips & Resources" from the American Civil Liberties Union (ACLU) offers resources on various topics for effective advocacy. www.aclu.org/advocacy-tips-resources

- "Effective Advocacy: Lessons from successful campaigns" from Stand provides examples of successful advocacy campaigns and the strategies they employed. www.stand.earth/publication/effective-advocacy-lessons-successful-campaigns

## Educational Institutions for Advocacy

- Kennedy School of Government at Harvard University provides courses on leadership, organizing, and advocacy. www.hks.harvard.edu

- The Ginsberg Center at the University of Michigan offers resources and support for students interested in advocacy and activism. ginsberg.umich.edu/article/advocacy-activism

Advocacy and activism are essential to promoting change and confronting the challenges of institutionalized racism. Engaging in advocacy, activism, and supporting organizations that do this work can make a significant difference. Remember, everyone has a role to play, and every effort, no matter how small, contributes to the more substantial movement for justice and equality.

# Research and Studies

Understanding the impact of racism and institutionalized racism is deeply rooted in scholarly research and studies. They provide objective insights and robust data that can help us understand the depth of the problem and point toward potential solutions. Here are some resources to find academic papers, case studies, and the latest research on racism and institutionalized racism.

## Academic Papers on Racism and Institutionalized Racism

- Google Scholar is a comprehensive resource for scholarly literature across various publishing formats and disciplines. Use keywords such as "racism," "institutionalized racism," "systemic racism," etc. scholar.google.com

- JSTOR is a digital library for scholars, researchers, and students. It provides access to thousands of academic journals, books, and primary sources. www.jstor.org

- PubMed comprises over thirty-two million citations for biomedical literature from MEDLINE, life science journals, and online books. Useful for research on health disparities and racial bias in healthcare. pubmed.ncbi.nlm.nih.gov

## Case Studies

- The case collection at Harvard Business School includes a series of case studies on race, work, and leadership. www.hbs.edu/faculty/units/leadership/Pages/case-collection.aspx

- Kirwan Institute for the Study of Race and Ethnicity offers numerous research and policy briefs, including case studies. kirwaninstitute.osu.edu/research

- Race Forward's research section includes numerous case studies on racial justice issues. www.raceforward.org/research

- SAGE Publications publishes academic content and case studies in various disciplines, including sociology and racial studies. us.sagepub.com/en-us/nam/home

## Latest Research Findings

- The American Psychological Association (APA) publishes the latest research findings in the field of psychology, including studies on the psychological impact of racism. www.apa.org

- The Pew Research Center conducts public opinion polling, demographic research, media content analysis, and other empirical social science research, including studies on race and ethnicity. www.pewresearch.org/topics/race-and-ethnicity

- The Racial Equity Tools are a resource to inspire and facilitate conversations, strategies, and actions to help people achieve racial equity. www.racialequitytools.org/research

- Urban Institute provides the latest research and policy analyses on race, ethnicity, and the ongoing fight for equity. www.

urban.org/policy-centers/cross-center-initiatives/race-and-ethnicity-policy

Research and studies are vital for challenging our preconceptions and grounding our understanding of racism and institutionalized racism in facts and evidence. They enable us to confront these issues in informed, impactful ways. We encourage you to explore these resources and apply the knowledge gained to your parenting strategies, advocacy efforts, and personal growth.

# Empowerment and Resilience

Navigating through this journey of parenthood is far from easy, and the complexities of raising Black children in a society steeped in institutionalized racism can feel overwhelming. But remember, you are not alone, and resources are available to support and guide you every step of the way.

In this resource guide, we've curated an array of tools, information, and networks to help empower you. From books that broaden perspectives, to podcasts that spark insights, to helplines ready for your call, these resources aid your quest to raise confident, successful, and resilient sons.

Remember that this guide does not offer one-size-fits-all solutions, but a compass designed to guide you in your unique journey. As you explore these resources, take what resonates with you and adapt it to your personal needs and situations. Your wisdom, paired with these resources, will create the most powerful tool in the fight against institutionalized racism.

Your role as a parent is of utmost significance. You are the first line of defense and the primary source of love, guidance, and education for your children. Together, with the support of these resources, you are fostering a generation of Black men who are resilient, confident, and prepared to challenge the systemic issues they face.

Continue to learn, grow, and connect. Each step forward, however small, is a victory. And always remember—the love, resilience, and strength you impart to your sons are the most potent weapons against their challenges. Our collective effort and commitment to raising the next generation will shape a brighter, more equitable future for all.

# Acknowledgements

Thanks to Clyde McElvene, to Patricia Elam Ruff, to my husband, Joe Murray, and to my agent, Carol Mann, who read early drafts of this manuscript and provided enormously helpful conversations and dialogues. I thank as well Ella Ross, Terrance Brown, Joyce Ladner, Marc Richardson, James and Lonise Bias, and others for allowing me to invade their lives, secrets, and thoughts. I thank them for the trust they gave, which I sought diligently not to abuse as I told their story and mine.

# About the Author

Marita Golden is a veteran teacher of writing and an acclaimed award-winning author of over twenty works of fiction, nonfiction, and anthologies. As a teacher of writing, she has served as a member of the faculties of the MFA Graduate Creative Writing Programs at George Mason University and Virginia Commonwealth University and in the MA Creative Writing Program at Johns Hopkins University. As a literary consultant, she offers writing workshops, coaching, and manuscript evaluation services.

Books by Marita Golden include: the novels *The Strong Black Woman: How a Myth Endangers the Physical and Mental Health of Black Women*, *The Wide Circumference of Love*, *After*, and *The Edge of Heaven*; the memoirs *Migrations of the Heart* and *Don't Play in the Sun: One Woman's Journey Through the Color Complex*; and the anthology *Us Against Alzheimer's: Stories of Family Love and Faith*. She is the recipient of many awards, including the Writers for Writers Award presented by Barnes & Noble and Poets and Writers, an award from the Authors Guild, and the Fiction Award for her novel *After* from the Black Caucus of the American Library Association.

As a literary activist, Marita cofounded and serves as President Emerita of the Zora Neale Hurston/ Richard Wright Foundation.